HONGYUN

New and Collected Shorter Poems, 1955-2005

By

J. Michael Yates

authorHOUSE

1663 Liberty Drive, Suite 200
Bloomington, Indiana 47403
(800) 839-8640
www.AuthorHouse.com

© 2005 J. Michael Yates. All Rights Reserved.

No part of this book may be reproduced, stored in a retrieval system, or transmitted by any means without the written permission of the author.

First published by AuthorHouse 03/22/05

ISBN: 1-4208-5205-1 (e)
ISBN: 1-4208-2770-7 (sc)

Library of Congress Control Number: 2005900589

Printed in the United States of America
Bloomington, Indiana

This book is printed on acid-free paper.

Credit:
Cover painting by Royal Hocking
Cover design by Nicole Jang
Author photo by Hongyun Chen

PRAISE FOR THE WORKS OF THE AUTHOR

"When Yates and I first met and lunched at the University of Missouri, he was an undergraduate. His work was brilliant then. This I told him and his department head. This *Canticle for Electronic Music* of his endorses my fortune telling capacities."—W. H. Auden, *QUEST*

"When we had lunch with Zbigniew and Bogdan, I forgot to thank you (and Enzenzberger) for help with that Creeley dust-up in Montreal over Robinson Jeffers. I appreciate your keeping me out of trouble almost as much as I appreciate your work."—Czeslaw Milosz

"I appreciate this poet's concentration, swiftness, density: his choice for the deeply personal utterance, and that only. He wastes no time with exercises, set themes, and other conventional maneuvers."— Henry Rago, editor *Poetry*

"Each word is beautifully set, and in many of them the effect of the whole poem is of gentle flooding light—as of a honeycomb breaking and dissolving in the mind."—Keith Harrison, *Canadian Literature*

"This young writer, unlike most, is fearless in matters of dangerous themes and dialogue which will come clearly over the lights." Arthur Miller (as judge of Yates' Major Hopwood Award winning manuscript, *Subjunction*)

"With great admiration for your work."—Joyce Carol Oates

"...a wonder—a book of rich, round clarities which can be read from beginning to end like a novel or opened anywhere and sampled at random. Whatever way it is read, the result is enjoyment and understanding, and awe."—John Newlove of *Schedules of Silence,* winner of the Writer's Choice Award, Arts Festival, 1987 Winter Olympics.

"A few artists, like eagles, look full into the blaze of everything, transforming it and being transformed by it till chaos is defused and a new order is fused from the struggle. They risk pain and madness, but they live and are poets. If they find the right words they are great poets who in their work offer a transfigured universe where all can live for a time in safety or use as a launching post for new voyages of their own."—Fred Cogswell

"In the frozen, colorless landscapes and the 'mad light' of the aurora, he finds a full mystery and a barbaric absence at the same time: for Yates it resembles the inner space of awareness, a territory he has always explored brilliantly." —Marni Jackson, *The Toronto Star*

"He is violent and unpredictable…has a wild, unconventional imagination…"—James Dickey

"Dangerous minds investigate dangerous places in the mind. Most of your work lives in these places."—Yehuda Amichai

"Yates is singular in that he writes like himself; he has no leaders, no fellow travelers… He lives on intimate terms with fact and imagination—the result is this rare purity of language."—Charles Lillard, *The Malahat Review*

"Michael Yates is a great poet who has given us such a universe. I consider his Great Bear Lake Meditations to be by far the most ambitious and successful meditative poem ever written in Canada, and his other work falls short not in excellence but in scope of that masterpiece. In his hands, rhythms and words have resonances that vibrate to the farthest shores of consciousness." —Fred Cogswell

"If the other Yeats had read the poetry of this Yates, he'd have put down his pen and gone to bed early."—John Newlove

"There is a world of shadows and darkness in Yates' dream-like landscapes, often a mysterious darkness and sombreness of tones; at other times there is a cold brilliance of colors…often distracting, sometimes coldly silent and awesome, sometimes disturbing in their timelessness."—Glen A. Sorestad

"Superbly inventive, witty, profound, and disturbing, these [stories]…clearly establish J. Michael Yates as one of the most lively and original writers of his generation. This is a book to read and reread with increasing delight at the subtlety of its structures and the power of its insight. It is a book to keep and to quote from." —Robin Skelton

"An all-or-nothing writer with a beautifully alert intelligence."—Al Purdy

"Yates evokes the primal sense of wonder."—Ronald B. Hatch, *UofT Quarterly*

"One of the most lively and original writers of his generation."—Robin Skelton

"I find it the voice of my age."—George Jonas

"Mike Yates is usually ahead of other poets. What he writes about, how he goes about it—most of us couldn't hope to write for another ten years. Now, with *Nothing Speaks for the Blue Moraines*, he anticipates poets like Merwin and Stafford. The three of them have grown into their land, and set out the increasingly abstract and tenuous lines we must follow, if we're to have a chance at sanity and survival in North America. Yates is the best abstract poet I've read."— William L. Fox, *West Coast Poetry Review*

"Yates reminds us that we have no answers, only questions and guesses. It is one thing to look into the abyss. It is another thing when the abyss looks back."—Robert Hunter, *The Vancouver Sun*

"Writing a bad poem is very easy. Almost anybody can do it, and damned near everybody does. Writing a good poem is virtually impossible. One of the few people in this country who can do it is J. Michael Yates."—George Jonas

"What a beautiful title: Breath of the Snow Leopard. And what a great imagination gives breath to the book. Mike Yates again brings to life our emotional geography; passionately internalizes our landscape. This snow leopard leaps straight out of the permanence of its own sensual myth."—Ralph Gustafson

"Has a unique way of responding to the world"—John Robert Colombo

"A truly extraordinary man…one hell of a poet."—Peter Gzowski, *Morningside*, CBC network

"It is rare to come across a book that one can, with absolute certainty, place immediately on the shelf reserved for works one cannot do without."—Robin Skelton in the *Victoria Daily Times*

"If Yates's work isn't trend-setting, it will be because other writers won't be able to match it."—Andreas Schroeder in *The Vancouver Province*

"I consider *The Great Bear Lake Meditations* and *Nothing Speaks for the Blue Moraines* the two finest books of poetry published in Canada in the past thirty years."—Fred Cogswell

PARTS OF THIS BOOK HAVE APPEARED IN THE FOLLOWING:

BOOKS

Spiral of Mirrors (Golden Quill Press)

Hunt in An Unmapped Interior (Golden Quill Press)

The Great Bear Lake Meditations (Oberon)

Parallax (Sono Nis Press)

Nothing Speak for the Blue Moraines (Sono Nis Press)

Breath of the Snow Leopard (Sono Nis Press)

Various Northerly Meditations (League of Canadian Poets)

Insel: The Queen Charlotte Islands Meditations (Penumbra Press)

PERIODICALS

The Alaska Review, The Angels, Artscanada, Barataria, Beyond Baroque, Black and White, The British Columbia Library Quarterly, The caCANADAdada Review, Canadian Forum, Canadian Literature, Canadian Poetry Review, Carleton Miscellany, Cave (New Zealand), Chelsea, The Chicago Review, Crosscurrents, The Dalhousie Review, Discovery (Cathay Pacific Airlines), Edge (New Zealand), Edge Magazine, Expression (England), Familia (Romania), The Far Point, The Fiddlehead, Forum, Grain, Greenfield Review, The Hudson's Bay Company Canadian Poets Series, The Hudson Review, Interstate, The Kansas City Star, The Kenyon Review, The Little Magazine, The Lunatic Gazette, The Mad River Review, The Malahat Review, The Minnesota Review, Moana, Mundus Artium, The New Orleans Review, The New Yorker, The North American Poetry Review, The Northward Journal, The Ontario Review, Open Places, The Pacific Rim Quarterly, The Paris Review, The Peak, P.E.N. America, Poet (Madras), Poet and Critic, Poetry (Chicago) ("The

Ice Rider," "It Hardly Matters," "The Scorpion"), Poetry Australia, Poetry Northwest, The Ponchartrain Review, Prism International, Quarry, Quartet, The Quest, Rendezvous, The Riverside Review, Sage, Saturday Night, Secant, The Southern Review, Talon, The Tamarack Review, Trace, The Transatlantic Review, Tri-Quarterly, The Ubyssey, The University of Windsor Review, The University Review, The Vancouver Sun, Voices, The Wascana Review, The West Coast Poetry Review, The West Coast Review.

ANTHOLOGIES

Antologia De La Poesie Actual Canadiense Inglesa, ed. & trans. Betanzos-Santos (Universidad Artonoma, Mexico); Breve, ed. & trans. Pettinella (Mondadori, Roma); Colombo's Canadian Quotations, ed. Colombo (Hurtig); Contemporary Poetry of British Columbia, ed. Yates (Sono Nis); How Do I Love Thee, ed. Colombo (Hurtig); How Does a Poem Mean, ed. Ciardi (Houghton-Mifflin); Imagine Seeing You Here, ed. Charlesworth (Oxford University Press); In Youth, ed. Kostelanetz (Ballantine/Random); Intelegind Zapada, ed. & trans. Teodorescu & Negosanu (Editura Univers, Bucaresti); Made in Canada, ed. Lochhead & Souster (Oberon); Marked By The Wild, ed. Littlejohn & Pearce (McClelland & Stewart); Mirrors, ed. Pearce (Gage); The New Oxford Book of Canadian Verse, ed. Atwood (Oxford University Press); New: West Coast, ed. Candelaria (West Coast Review. Intermedia); Notes Toward a Native Land, ed. Wainwright (Oberon); Poeti Canadieni Contemporani (de limba engleza), ed. & trans. Caraion (Editura Albatros, Bucaresti), The Poets of Canada, ed. Colombo (Hurtig); The Poet's View, ed. Whitley (American Weave Press); Quingumbo: nova poesia norte-americana, ed. Keys, trans. Damasceno (Escrita, Sao Paulo); "Quotations from English Canadian Literature," ed. Strickland (Modern Canadian Library); Rhymes and Reasons, ed. Colombo (Holt, Rinehart & Winston); Skookum Wawa, ed. Geddes (Oxford University Press); Solo Flight, ed. McGillicutty (Resource Publications); To Say the Least, ed. Page (Press Porcepic), Water, ed. Carver (Peter Martin Associates); Western Windows, ed. Ellis (ComCept Press).

BROADCAST

The Canadian Broadcasting Corporation ("Ideas", "Anthology", "The Hornby Collection"); Societé Radio Canada; WDSU (New Orleans); Westdeutscher Rundfunk (Koln); Norddeutscher Rundfunk (Hamburg); Saarlandischer Rundfunk (Saarbrucken); Algemeene Vereeniging Radio Omroep (Amsterdam); A.L.M.O. (Antwerpen); Radio Tel Aviv; Radiodiffusion (France); N.H.K. (Tokyo); R.A.I. (Rome); Radiodiffusion Television Algerienne (Algiers); Radiodiffusion-Television Belge (Brussels); Osterreichischer Rundfunk (Vienna); Sender Freies Berlin (Berlin); Radio Nacional (Buenas Aires); Hessischer Rundfunk (Frankfurt).

WEB

AVALON magazine [Maudlin Press, featured for several months, poetry and fiction, ongoing]; **The HORSETHIEF'S JOURNAL** [Cayuse Press, featured presently and in fall and winter issues]; **WRITER'S BLOCK NEWSLETTER. WRITER'S CHOICE LITERARY JOURNAL, BORN MAGAZINE. ELECTICA MAGAZINE, POET'S CORNER , THE ALSOP REVIEW (Permanent Gallery), OCTAVO, SUBMISSION, ECLECTICA, GREEN TRICYCLE, BORN MAGAZINE, CENOTAPH, ALEXANDRIA DIGITAL LITERATURE, ZEROZINE,** Photographs at various sites.

* "Suggestion of Time Past," "Automobile Accident," "The Ice Rider," and "Lioness Tiergarten" appeared in the 1964 Major Hopwood award winning manuscript, "Inside the Grape," University of Michigan at Ann Arbor.

xii

For Hongyun, Myron, and Kavan

xiv

OTHER WORKS BY THE SAME AUTHOR

SPIRAL OF MIRRORS (poetry)

HUNT IN AN UNMAPPED INTERIOR (poetry)

CANTICLE FOR ELECTRONIC MUSIC (poetry)

MAN IN THE GLASS OCTOPUS (fiction)

THE GREAT BEAR LAKE MEDITATIONS (prose poems)

PARALLAX (prose poems)

CONTEMPORARY POETRY OF BRITISH COLUMBIA (editor)

THE ABSTRACT BEAST (fiction, drama, radio drama)

VOLVOX: Poetry from the Unofficial Languages o f Canada in

English Translation (editor)

NIGHT FREIGHT (drama)

NOTHING SPEAKS FOR THE BLUE MORAINES (poetry)

QUARKS: THREE PLAYS (drama)

THE CALLING (drama)

BREATH OF THE SNOW LEOPARD (poetry)

THE QUALICUM PHYSICS (poetry)

ESOX NOBILIOR NON ESOX LUCIUS (poetry)

FAZES IN ELSEWHEN (fiction)

FUGUE BRANCUSI (poetry)

PHENOMENOLOGY OF THE SPACE/TIME JAZZ (philosophy)

VARIOUS NORTHERLY MEDITATIONS (prose poems)

INSEL: The Queen Charlotte Islands Meditations (prose poems)

OITA POEMAS (poetry)

THE COMPLETELY COLLAPSIBLE PORTABLE MAN (poems)

SCHEDULES OF SILENCE (poems)

TORQUE (fiction 1960-1987, vol I)

TORPOR (fiction 1960-1987, vol II)

LINE SCREW: My Twelve Riotous Years Working Behind Bars in Some of Canada's Toughest Jails (memoir)

DURING: A Book of Interrogatives (philosophy)

I just do it.

—Alvin Jang

Just because you can doesn't mean you have to.

—John Skapski.

Whatever is truly wondrous and fearful in man never yet was put into words or books

—Herman Melville

xviii

TABLE OF CONTENTS

PRAISE FOR THE WORKS OF THE AUTHOR v

PARTS OF THIS BOOK HAVE APPEARED IN THE
FOLLOWING: ix

OTHER WORKS BY THE SAME AUTHOR xv

SCORPION 1

LANGUAGE 3

THREE LINES TWICE 4

CIVILIZED 5

POEM 6

UNTITLED 7

IT HARDLY MATTERS 8

MARIA 9

THE ICE RIDER 12

GODS, MEN, AND ALSO 14

LIONESS TIERGARTEN 15

LYNX-EYES 16

SUGGESTION OF TIME PAST 17

THE RECORDING 18

ALOGOS 20

VULTURES 21

GARDEN AFTER DARK 23
    Encoils me this year of the locust 23
    The locusts cover the land 23

In the burning light...23
Like light on a black wing 24
Thrust through the humid horizon?..................................24
It is a locust year...24
I think I remember dark voices in evening trees................24

REVERSAL 25

PURE PASSAGE 26

SOON 27

SCAVENGERS..29

VOICE 30

TWO DIMENSIONS..31

SLOUGH: THE DAYS 32

It is the lantern swinging too slowly between the word and the
light 32
The slow black desultory 32
Cedar light 33
Pause...33
Day with dangerous edges 34
The day that 35
prefer it return..35
Today..36
All weather is useful..37
Sangre de Cristo day..38
The day today..38
Day 39
Blessed are the high trees 39
Today..40
The whole of the day 41
All day and into...43
Day like a field 44
Mixing and multiplying 45

This day is my habitat..46

Between 46

Metamorphoses of black..47

Not even in time 48

More often now 49

Between dawn and dusk...51

Shut up 51

After I finished fearing...52

One day the parasite is 54

This is the truth..54

At the end of hope 55

Forgive me 56

I had been trying to discover 57

BURN TISSUE CYCLE 58

A long green laze 58

The men going as far north as they can go 58

The trees of heaven 59

Any scientist will tell you...59

A large fire at the centre...60

The embering logs of the vanished..61

I burned up my space 61

Sleep until it's alright 62

In a city of masts and fumes 63

AUTOMOBILE ACCIDENT..64

NOTHING TROJAN NOR GREEK 65

ONE HIEROGLYPH 66

THE CAVERN...67

ICE CARNIVAL...70

FERNWEH 72

ONE AFTERNESS OF WAR 74

xxi

GLASS AMOEBA 76

AIR MOVING 77

HUNT IN AN UNMAPPED INTERIOR 78
  A madman lost...78
  Cold game trails 78
  Face for a..79
  Lean sheep 79
  The bear 79
  What is it?...80
  His madness 80

APPROACH..81

SENTRY..83

ONE IMMOBILE NOON 85

EMERGENCE OF AN EYE 86

DEATH OF A FISH 88

LOCUST SPRING..89

EARLY SUMMER..90

THE SEASONAL..91

ARACHNID 93

THIRD EYE...94

AFTER 95

A MATHEMATICS 96

WHEN WOLVES 97

WAY INTO WINTER 99

TRANSPARENCY OF BLACKNESS...........................100
  If there is nothing..100
  The humour of a wilderness 100

One wants his own way...100

Outside me 101

And here, something rising...101

DOCTRINE 102

There is some chance..102

HUNTER...103

The animals approach too near now 103

PRELUDE..104

Black trees on the shore..104

WHALE 105

When the darkness appears just a little darker 105

GOOD TO SAY..106

I think it might be good to say 106

DRIVING 107

I must remain close to myself in these times 107

EVENT HORIZON VERNAL.....................................109

When the dewdrop door yawns....................................109

THERE WILL BE NO MORE PASSENGERS 110

There will be no more passengers.................................110

THIRTEEN 112

When the blind bulls of light 112

ISOTHERM THIRTY-SIX 114

If you glimpse my body-heat.......................................114

THE KNOWING 115

The dark owls roosting in the yellow acacia 115

SIGN 116

Something wishes just to be what it is 116

xxiii

CEDAR WAXWING 117
    This is the centre 117

PHOENIX...118
    Not only can I not have the Phoenix without the ashes 118

SAPSUCKER..119
    All night I lay not listening to the cougar calling through black
    rain 119

SPARROW 120
    The insects are up 120

THE FLUME—YUN CYCLE I.......................................121
    The flowing of us..121

THE TIME—YUN CYCLE II 122
    The time is come 122

PREHISTORIC MEALS..123
    Faith like an eagle blinded 123

THE MOST INTELLIGENT CEPHALOPOD....................125
    In a fury of ink...125

FROM THE GREAT BEAR LAKE MEDITATIONS 126
    The wolves say to the dogs what the madman of me
    says to the...126
    The fish move with the winds, their sails under the
    currents under 126
    The totem poles are turned toward the river. Beneath
    these the...126
    First sense as I awaken under the fans of northern
    summer light:...126
    I awaken in a rage, with the exhaust of bitter warfare
    trailing through 126
    I persist in a little fabric between me and the world.
    This is the sleep 127

Legend: The God in the sun made two men. In the
hands of one..127

How long ago is it that my ancestors kept slaves?
What remains of..128

At least two rivers confluence inside me: one clear.
The substance..128

Say the word. *Skeena.* Say the words. *Skeena, Kispiox,
Stikeen, Babine.* 128

This is no ordinary piece of stone. In the rising firelight,
it was taken 129

Alcohol is what this village died of. When they made the
pubs legal for..129

Soon. *The fire or the storm.* Might as well burn now. When
the storm..129

How far north will a mind consent? I'm alive because
I wonder how...130

A bright scream of heat goes up from the landscape.
And then the...130

When am I? *Soon. Possibly. Consider the shape of the fountain.
Enter* 130

Teeth of air close upon the teeth of water. Between
circles a man in 131

There were some secrets I wished to conceal from the
wilderness,...131

How shall I contain fourteen hundred feet of water —
is there 131

I take today on a light line in fair weather: today, the
fish-shape, ...131

On this island too north for trees, I fish for arctic char.
The ice-blue...132

As I've made myself of alcohol, paper and computer circuitry,
these..132

I return here. Like a man who has bombed a city and
returns as a 133

These peaks which mouth the air of the distance jut nowhere
from 133

The first aurora of my life. I've been with a woman
and now this..133

That this town died of earthquake would be difficult
to guess, ...134

Geese arise in my inside skies when the wolf-pack
gathers in my..134

Something is rising in the black throat of the sky. Something
draws..134

And now, only one dread: I'll die before I've said all my
objections to..134

I'm here to remember my animal, that ghost-beast of many
shapes..135

Each hour I deposit another stone in the pack-sack
beneath which 135

Noah wasn't the first sad craft of stunned, delivered,
bitching..135

Beyond the wall of the boundless city, I seat myself.
On a stone. To..136

The opaque man closes doors carefully between rooms.
Now. There..136

Always, before I've seen the wolf, the wolf has seen me
twice. The..136

I'm coming soon to the end of me, to the edge, the drop-off,
to the 136

A gloomy peace. Pause between what nothing explains and
everyone..137

The tse-tse fly the man seeks through the streets of
dreamed and 137

Empty powerlines walk on stilts over my ridges.
Empty causeways..138

And so the barbarians came. Over the high walls
of my skull, they..138

The still dark figures in a line against the white
mountain are still 138

The hands in my head were fumbling, fumbling
with some last 138

xxvi

I haven't time, because the glacier dwindles
beneath this escalate 139

I am alive. Since the beginning. Long before the ice.
The muskoxen 139

I've been handled like a dangerous animal always.
I'm a dangerous..139

In, inward deeper now, light dies into the dark.
A blue-white ring 139

What points on the compass if all directions are equal,
if all directions..140

The faces of time are circular, the faces of space are
circular—and I,..140

Only the words which survive passage through silence,
only those..140

Where some unenvisaged things have vanished, there is
no passage. I 141

The beast who sleeps at the ends of the optic nerves,
stirs, wakens, ...141

Only the albino fish survives time, darkness, absence of eyes.
I must 141

An intentional amnesia causes the clarity of this aesthesia.
Have I 142

An eye alone in passage fangles laws with one end: to
break them. 142

Rams of the sea butt the sea-cliffs unenthusiastically.
West, the last..142

All my days to come are hung like drying char upon a pole.
To exceed 143

These are the poisoning grounds, here where the
birds nest at..143

I'm nothing who dreams the something with whom
the world dreams..143

Yes, the wise seething of these flies, as I come upon the
mandible of..144

I've been right here, in the air, without scaffolding,
turning expertly..144

xxvii

One totem demands: When the father grows feeble
and contributes no 144

Again and again I go away from you and send back
only words......145

I dream cautiously, as if between high peaks heavy
with avalanches. 145

A dredge like this can bite a mountain down. It eats almost 145

The moon is closer to the earth in the north of the northern ...146

Ideas decoyed and then out-stalked him. He lay at
night disbelieving 146

Daily she came less and less cautiously for the small
food I held in the 146

That earth turns, I have no objection, but how it
turns concerns me. 146

This is my receipt for death: I'm swimming hard in
arctic water, ...147

A man, warmly dressed, in perfect health, mushing his
dogs a short 147

Beaver. I become this: outraged by the perpendicularity
of the trees, ...147

I no longer believe in what I don't know about cities,
but there's 148

Today I've been a race of men - engineers, all of us,
aloft on the giddy 148

The salmon circle a spawn, crimson in clear emerald.
There's a time 148

At freeze-up and break-up the suicides occur. It's part
of the weather 149

FROM PARALLAX 150

Death like a parachute collapsing 150

Death like a parachute collapsing. 150

Death, too, is arrangement, ...150

There is at least one indestructible negative 150

The photograph come uncemented from its
dimensions is a man - 150

In this city of suicides and no storms, it is never hot nor
cold. I can 151

A small room gone strange with distances: my hand
engaged at a...151

Beneath a bridge of silence passes the night ferry:....................151

Light-leaks in the darkroom, the fungus of explanation. 152

I begin to notice the landscape which has always been
there. Always, ...152

Beyond black, worms of love-talk snarl in a ball
at the centre of 152

The infinity sign is ours: a hieroglyph whose
two worlds die into one...152

What grows out of blackness is still blackness. Light:
blackness out of..153

The last woman was a green light passing over my skin,
a rising 153

At once both sides of the lens constitutes one
reproduction or 153

Every radar is solitary: the presence made of
absences which navigates 154

Over the high peaks at the middle range, the
chartreuse flower of 154

The final camera's camera is the camera, the seeing
thing I don't see 154

Destructive, these creative loves exceed the sad seep of a
century over 155

Meanwhile you are dying and I am dying and we aren't
together. 155

I know by the sound of my breathing that it is no
longer within my..156

While eyes — gone green over the green glow of the
radar screen 156

FROM INSEL: THE QUEEN CHARLOTTE ISLANDS
MEDITATIONS 157

This winter in which you find me is not your winter 157

This winter in which you find me is not your winter..............157

Because things much more dangerous than death remain
unreined by...157

When the colourless hand of fog closes over the coast,
it is not death, ...157

Preferring to bide its opposite, things bide time instead...........157

Time to fangle, time to become a beach between at
least two more 157

There are choices: Become a larger fisherman. Or a
fisherman smaller..157

Begin fishing in deep winter. Go landless, navigate
your vessel away 157

At the capsize comes an easing of decision: when the
hands blue and 158

I can see more than one snowpeak from this beach.
Alaska. On a..158

You are forward. I am aft. Control of the outboard
engine is mine. 158

At the sandy graveside, looming thunderheads of
words close away 159

Child, may you never notice that seabirds, electrons,
and galaxies are..159

Pulse unsteady at the speed of dark....................................159

Don't let them do it under cover of darkness..........................160

This winter in which you find me is not my winter..................160

What lingers here still hushes and gives on the wind: 160

At sudden places, through this tree-tunnelled way
toward Rose Spit 160

Now and then the citizen wins a battle. Reluctantly.
Humbly. But the 160

No, not innocence, I have not come north again
to recover an..161

Island north is new and not new to me. What is new,
perhaps, lives...161

xxx

Time and tide, exhaling here, now, after the long
breathing-in of 161

What enters the amber eye of the cormorant never
reaches an organ 161

Those who come to these islands come in fright, come
from 162

Like geese and teal and widgeon and certain other
animals of water 162

Evidence of my having been somewhere sometimes
takes on the 162

Flight was never a way of life. Neither was life in
the nesting...162

I don't remember the rest, but her letter thus came to
the end of 162

Flight is the solitary goose-cry in the night of being
frightened of all 162

Getting elsewhere is one way of not staying and,
with luck, not...162

Out of flight, I try and again try to coax a way of life. 163

Accidentally, I am blowing out the lantern of what
I know with the...163

Love of edge. Have lived it. Always I have lived
toward love of edge,...163

...I'm serious about the whales, Jack Gilbert 163

Fluke. Seamark for a vanishing point: thus, then,
these flukes fan, ...163

Lake surrounded by land surrounded by sea. 164

The mind swings like the needle of a compass
between sentences of 164

In this geography of north the language of north is
understood by 164

Here, it is possible to grow so preoccupied with the
detail of the 165

Far, deep, away in the south of my time alive, I
condense the many...165

xxxi

I have failed to cure my compass of north and the needle
no longer...165

He was one who had come to love dark. He surmised so.
And that he..166

North, deep north. Poseidon, landlord of water, skulks
the sands of...166

An oilslick translates itself from the surf to the sand
beneath his feet. 167

Only in angry rapture, might a god carve this voluptuous
killer...167

The ones here whose nicknames I learn, the ones who
die almost...167

It is not that island time means more dimly than all
other time. 167

Deeper than sapwood, I could become something
almost authentic..168

As the wharves zipper together land and water, hold on.
Hold it 168

Inside the dark body of the real, what I point to only
resembles what 169

Announce the environment has been settled: the dam
will go up on 169

What confirms life can kill. And will. 169

He loved wine. 170

I have been a war. 170

Footing once firm on the wharf gives the quick
twitch and sag of..170

In the sea-noon light, a strut falls away, beneath
a wharf built to...171

Nothing is behind it all. 171

Dear Outside:...172

Inside the river, rocks roll over and disclose their
dark, wet unders...172

When I touch selected surfaces: carved soapstone,
certain places of...172

xxxii

In the mind-light of braiding river time,
I was a minor incident...172

Follow this way through the dark curtain of rain.
It will take you 173

Here, beyond the small sand mountain at the edge
of the reserve, ...173

That dried black crop hanging up there above the stove?
Seaweed..173

Mind this: stick to the driftwood when you screw
around up near...173

It's an old picture, be careful, no, go ahead, count 'em,
twenty-seven 174

Whispers live still between the logs which shape the
vacancies of this..174

Sea otter carry the uncertain remainder of the species
within. Their 174

Gentian light domes the opaline inlet. Each instant: a
diatom of 175

A metabolism gone as still as stone, seemingly not breathing,
silent 175

This rising river of answers because I have no
Haida questions...175

From buried adzes, from a broken yew bow, from
strata of shell, they..175

Something not yet reported lost is dying with difficulty.
Starving..175

Hoar-frost whiskers the weather- silvered planking
of the wharf. The...176

One could come, here, to the death of wrath...........................176

This carving was one of numberless lights in the blood............176

The icecap of knowing somewhat remits...................................177

The droplet trapped in the spider skein rocks in thin
breeze like a bell 177

Capacity to dream an absolute shape of island
without means to 178

xxxiii

Infrequently, rage for an open place, for the camouflage
of visibility..178
To escape the island sickness, travel to the horizon,
turn left...178
Melting light. 178
Agate from pores of a basalt seafloor fall to the beach
over the 178
Vertical wind, horizontal rain, the affair of warm
Japanese current 179
The high-rigger tops a home-tree..179
Caution near the ones like winter eagles who pause
atop only the 179
Stonestroke..180
The stain of borrowed time does not wash nor wear
free from the 180
Lost is another word for ordinary in ordinary insular
speech. Islands..180
More than geography removed: of her, I remember
only eyelight. The 180
This dream of a captive will letting go: an old and
huge sailing craft, ...181
Easy, the thought gone dancing to celebrate, the
thought gone..181
Gauze sky of a maker contemplates its fake in the
one-way mirror of 181
There comes to me nothing to say on behalf of
space squandered in..181
I've come here to salvage, to terrorize a consciousness,
sunken hugely 182
For him, parts of island remain tidily *as though*
until he breaks parts 182
Tlell: 182
Night set. Remembrance of the future in wrath: this
chisel is chief...182

To this the spooked hope has come: the spell of
glacial refugium: a 183

Almost love of a kind for the animals and trees warily
enters my 183

I was numerous figures of time at the flumes. 183

The doors of gods are closed tight tonight. 184

The golden goose-horn of eternity. 184

I have availed myself of heat, of light, near the blaze
of your big...184

Here at the frontier, it turns suddenly the wrong weather for
those 185

Indeed there is a personal god up there. And nosey.............185

Interregnum between the twin lanterns of dusk and dawn.......185

Toward pure purpose:..186

Newcomer, take note of this: here the drunken
eagle flies with 186

A cage of white mainland birds, long captive,
unexpectedly freed...186

These words against the darkness from which
these words are carved. 186

These silences against the black fire inside which
all silence forges...186

So gracefully silent eternity shrills silence at the tiny,
temporal thrash. 186

The situation of fishing explains me: my high-seas trawlers,
the big...186

Gale winter raindark and only this wharf not listing................187

I was up foreword. She was in the galley fixing the grub.
The..187

A hamper of white mainland birds suddenly freed:
Will releases, ...187

She spent the time of her life insular, deliberating
what might be 187

Because north is nearest nothing, again and again
I come back,..187

xxxv

The glare sea of excess truth now surrounds
my used residue of...187

It is said it was a death-drive...188

I am 188

The fire which has been burning toward me forever
has arrived. And 189

He lived beneath the tyranny of a massive memory.
As he died he..189

Portrait of my fingerprints upon a snowy massif.
And my fingerprints 189

Tigerine stripes of first light across the dark moss
rainforest floor..189

I AM ALIVE...190

At a place of three-minded water, ...190

Don't slam the screen door of the dream as you leave. 192

DURING: A BOOK OF INTERROGATIVES 193

It must speak of things 193

HONGYUN

SCORPION

Who knows

The hot stung days

And brittle cold nights

Of keeping a great poison pure.

As if it weren't enough:

These blank eyes,

This useless armour,

Automatic claws that rasp—

Body that lives,

That lives apart from ... that other.

Come: gods, men, angels,

Who among you will think of me

When my night arrives,

When I rise over the dunes,

When the long neck of this

J. Michael Yates

Tail of mine draws back

To strike the heel

Of my only moon.

HONGYUN

LANGUAGE

Language is the small snake tongue

I flick out

To receive the body of the world.

J. Michael Yates

THREE LINES TWICE

Inside the river, rocks roll over

And disclose their dark, wet unders.

Beneath them, everything dies of travel and light.

Look up.

Check the geese.

Go the other way.

HONGYUN

CIVILIZED

I knew by the sudden silence

In the streets inside me

An animal had entered the clearing:

One soft paw upraised,

One precise ear followed

The sequence of closing shutters.

J. Michael Yates

POEM

It must speak of things

Which go quickly

Through shadows of consciousness

Like small animals in the thicket

You cannot quite

Be sure you've seen.

HONGYUN

UNTITLED

In the blood-coloured cage

Behind my ribs

The lion circles

In his chest

Turns a silhouette of slow rage

Like a man with a lion in his chest

J. Michael Yates

IT HARDLY MATTERS

It hardly matters now.

Now that the ring

Of bright blue

Violet fire horizon

Has gone out.

It hardly matters now

That the hedge of flame

I called "horizon" is gone,

That things that have always

Mattered have never mattered.

That it hardly matters

Now and now and now

Is a golden animal

That glows almost

In this tightening dark.

HONGYUN

MARIA

Within her purple goblet,

Maria swims.

Outside the world condenses.

She doesn't miss anything anymore.

Events turn on the crystal curve

Or escape altogether her senses.

Things are too much without us,

I said, just over the sill of sense.

She went.

My words went after her.

Darkly. In waves. Like a plague of insects.

Half the next afternoon

I watched a poisoned ant

Reel along a table-edge.

Dreadful to see time passing in the distance.

Worse: to see nothing,

Hear its whistle. Only.

J. Michael Yates

A tear slid

Between her eye

And sight.

I thought all along

She was one of those women who pass through a cloud

Through your life a bird through space.

Memory, my old egg,

Broke upon my head,

Dripped into my eyes.

My mind's reach groped for her

A hand in the dark

For a key before a door.

Unable not to stand her any longer

I came with the murderous vengeance of a child

And a madman's innocence.

HONGYUN

When I race my wet finger

Around her goblet-lip,

She — or the glass itself — sings like a violin.

J. Michael Yates

THE ICE RIDER

Inside me

At the shore of the frozen lake

They are still talking.

We shouted, shouted,

Waved our dim lanterns over the snow.

I feel him riding through the darkness over the ice.

They say

The centre is a deep unfreezing maw.

Beneath the horse the ice mumbles and moans.

The hag scratches and suspects.

Through her snow of remembered disappointments

She curses him laughing in a warm room up the shore.

HONGYUN

Won't he go 'round? the boy began.

Eyes like frozen lakes with dark centres

Stopped him short.

This is one

Of many, many villages

Snowed apart around a frozen lake.

In the spring

Gone are ice, ice village, eye-like frozen lake.

And ice riders riding over the ice through the dark.

It is winter,

I listen into the wind

For hooves, for a splash, for a shout.

J. Michael Yates

GODS, MEN, AND ALSO

Metaphor is centaur

Part one thing

Part everything

Thing is thing

And many other things

This speaks

Of how I live

Of how I die

A man and a horse

Have blood and breath

There is no April in Heaven

HONGYUN

LIONESS TIERGARTEN

Fixed on the smoky agate of her eye,

We are embarred and blankly watching.

Gone finally is the thing that paces,

First from blood, then from merely pacing.

Glare, which takes us in a blur of tawny

And a shadow-zebra of bars,

Past your misty mask of yellow

Thinly simmering a ruse,

Past embers of dermis lemon,

Beyond incremental pools

Of hot transitional chartreuse…

Into a deep, deep smouldering lagoon,

Round and full of green and dying moons

And spiral echoes of jungle afternoons.

J. Michael Yates

LYNX-EYES

High,

Russet-eyed,

Full of fire

And the scent of green,

Swiftly, drowsily,

She closes about me

As summer spaces

Close about

The last ungathered

Floes of spring.

Tell the stone-eyed Eumenides:

"He vanishes

Into the eyes

Of a great soft-eyed Lynx."

HONGYUN

SUGGESTION OF TIME PAST

Room to room

Her woman's home

Was a woman's purse

Of pungences, extended.

A tomb of all the auras

Of all the things

A woman puts

Between herself and world.

Pennies from a moist hand,

Dry tobacco, dense perfume

Resuscitate someone earlier

For nose, memory, and room.

J. Michael Yates

THE RECORDING

Around the round, flat disc of dark

Needles of light are wounding through.

Around the moon transcriptions turn,

Turn against me,

Turn against

A dull point pressed to an old track.

Inward, inward, moves the groove

Until the blunt dagger knifes the moon.

Between forefinger and the thumb,

The moon's scar

Is a wound across a fingerprint:

The scratch a shadow-tree grates

Across smooth grooves of lake.

HONGYUN

Go softly in the moon-coloured grass;

Steps upon a sidewalk rasp:

Warped platter, limping, stuck,

Spindled in this heirloom phonograph.

J. Michael Yates

ALOGOS

Still day

fragile day

I am all

the

light there is

today

HONGYUN

VULTURES

A wavering pillar of vultures

Rises like dark smoke

From a distant point on this plain.

Here, even

The rocks

Eat one another.

When my stomach lifts and plunges

In the thermal currents of steady noon,

I know the vultures are poising.

Beneath a porous animal skull,

A lizard bulges his eyes into the humidity.

The sand swallows his color.

When the wedge of birds pierces the horizon,

The earth will swell and fall open

In two parched clods. Then the gods

J. Michael Yates

Will descend, nudging, flogging one another,

Clacking their dry beaks through all space

For this very little of theirs.

HONGYUN

GARDEN AFTER DARK

I

Line of western progress,

Circle of eastern return,

The spiral arises out of itself,

II

Encoils me this year of the locust.

Scholars' backs, bent once

Into questions, stiffen into whips.

III

The locusts cover the land

With a dense fog

Of their grinding.

IV

In the burning light

The brilliant insects continue,

Concealed from the vision changing

J. Michael Yates

V

Like light on a black wing.

When last were there words

Behind the silent lightning

VI

Thrust through the humid horizon?

Words lost in the mountains

Never, perhaps, return.

VII

It is a locust year;

That is perhaps return - though

The fruit trees do not bloom in dark voices:

VIII

I think I remember dark voices in evening trees.

Nothing exists, at last, for a moment,

But I enter its garden on a night of no moon.

HONGYUN

REVERSAL

The shadow

Of a bird settled an instant

On the transparent twig

Behind her eyes.

Then flew.

Now All my journeys

Begin at their destinations.

I shall

Climb this violet mountain

From its snow-summit down.

J. Michael Yates

PURE PASSAGE

Antlers grow inward

Within this skull:

Enmesh, contend,

Darken, fall

Velvet somewhere

     empty

HONGYUN

SOON

Through

Rainy silence,

Silent darkness,

The sullen heave

Beneath dark water

Of roiling stones.

River I have lived

Beside always, deepening,

Raving with its mountains

Toward the center of the earth.

Perhaps I might have known:

Hot light too close upon the glacier,

Avalanches in the distance,

One lean ram poised just after evening

On a high crag alone.

J. Michael Yates

What is this

Swinging slowly

To a close?

HONGYUN

SCAVENGERS

After the blood has dried

And the wind is overcome

In the deep weeds, flies

Conquer the earth

With their blackness,

Their wide seething.

The killing is past.

Reek and bones and flies

Are left to the misshapen

And the slow of wing.

In a rage of insects,

Scavengers fiercely swill

Remains of the greater animal:

Flesh they cannot kill.

J. Michael Yates

VOICE

Voice comes to me

Through a thicket of willows

At the end of a viper-green neck.

It is the small lantern

Swinging too slowly

Between the word and the light.

No matter what takes me to

Deep stream-beds of all blood:

I'm awake beneath these stones.

HONGYUN

TWO DIMENSIONS

The shadow of my hand

Reaches forth and imprints

This wilderness of fewer and fewer words.

Something remains concealed always

Some shrunken life, a brute remoteness,

A half-breathing beneath deep snow.

Silence between winter peaks is incomplete,

And the gun-shot, and just after:

Nothing emerges but in trialogue.

Darkness displaces outline first in the narrow valley.

For a long time after my outline disappears, snow-crests

In the distance continue to turn in pink light.

J. Michael Yates

SLOUGH: THE DAYS

I

It is the lantern swinging too slowly between the word and the light.

It is the lantern swinging too slowly between the world and the light.

It is the light swinging too slowly between the world and the word.

II

The slow black desultory

of spring streaming

between banks of snow

vanishing openly

going where things which vanish

all things do vanish

going and going where

all things which vanish

all of it vanishes

all things

go

HONGYUN

III

Cedar light

green conifer air

inside day

low cabin fever

I am here

and could not be here

possibly

IV

Pause

because

There is rising pain

in the heart

of the day

spreading like rings

—from a stone thrown

into the sea—

toward the horizons

J. Michael Yates

toward the farthest

membranes

of the chest cavity

of the day

toward the weakest

chink

of the caulkwork

in

the high cabin

walls

V

Day with dangerous edges

Like the edges of a broken

Stained-glass shade.

The day takes a pill,

The edges dull.

The lethal edges.

HONGYUN

Also the edges

Which carve an idea

Of day almost perfectly

Through variegated glass.

VI

The day that

Could not be

but is

is

And has arrived

from a source

less palpable

than dream

I

prefer it return

the way it came

It has amnesia

Or has grown too old

in transit to recall

as once it could

J. Michael Yates

Or

have

I

VII

Today

in me

things exist only in another way

I turn to someone

to explain

There is an uneasy

pause

I ask instead what

weather

is

expected

HONGYUN

VIII

All weather is useful

for something

something thrifty in me

suggests.

Simply match the activity

to the weather.

What activity was it

that I had in mind?

Nothing

Precisely nothing

What weather is it precisely

That precise nothing

requires?

J. Michael Yates

IX

Sangre de Cristo day
No closer than the words
No closer ever than
the words.

X

The day today
Is not out the window

not

in gazing out the window

at the high bladed

landscape

not

in exceeding the pane

to be

among two mountain squirrels

and

and one flame-headed

black woodpecker

none of them making their

expected and limited noises.

XI

Day

is between and beneath

these

colourless computer keys

persist

penetrate the day

seep down in between

Q

and

A

XII

Blessed are the high trees

with their heads in the mist

J. Michael Yates

nothing to try to see

nothing to sense

blessed more the rocks

about tree line

with nothing moving through

them.

XIII

Today

Very, very fluorescent

green sails

three, the third, damaged

On an invisible line

Between dark sky

and

darker sea

HONGYUN

I am a cursor moving

across

low and lowering

across and across

the phospor green

computer screen

The more motionless

I sit

The harder and louder

heart's anvil

strikes and rings

It is power-failure

I'm

waiting for

XIV

The whole of the day

hiding inside

the skin

of the grizzly bear

J. Michael Yates

Looking out through

the eyes of the dead animal

the landscape, animate and still

is, by turns, comic and

target

awaiting psychotic

attack.

Sense of silvertip immensity,

I stand and reach tall on

On the conifer,

For a moment, wish these

claws retractable,

then rip the bark high overhead.

Look upon that signal,

Ozymandias,

and despair.

HONGYUN

XV

All day and into

the arctic dark

The wind sounded

Of a herd of buffalo

Grazing outside the white

Cook tent full of the

Picnic table, warm yukon stove,

And me.

J. Michael Yates

I didn't look. Pissed out

the tent-flap without looking

For fear that the herd

loosed 300 miles from

the nearest road

by madmen

would metamorphose

into something less hungry

but more intelligent

and with sense of destructive

humour

XVI

Day like a field

of

finned ice

all of blinding whiteness

and waiting laceration

HONGYUN

This is not a white

built of

colours which taken together

imply

rainbow

hoodoos

among which a day

loses itself

without sound.

XVII

Mixing and multiplying

the death and life

about me,

the fabric of this light

has this feel

to the fingertips

of seeing.

J. Michael Yates

XVIII

This day is my habitat

I shall want and want

I have wanted and wanted

It will make my lie

down under green pasture.

XIX

Between

the solitude

which

is

imperative

and

the lonliness

which is desperate

and

intolerable

HONGYUN

There should

be

something

XX

Metamorphoses of black:

the hunting grebes

in the shadow of the sailboat

whose shadow rocks at mooring

as my shadow rocks at evening

mooring, the dark now falling

faster than ever before.

The darkening darkness in my

mouth showing more

than ever before

around the parts of the grin

widening wider than ever

before

J. Michael Yates

XXI

Not even in time

Will you come to understand

That there is one side

To a story

The one being told

This

How many sides at once

Can you hear

Nor learn that

You must hear all sides of

A story

To determine

It was not worth hearing

At all

HONGYUN

Not what was told

Nor finally

Even how

It requires many lifetimes

To hear all sides of one

Story with only an average

Number of sides

Although it must be said that

men increase the numbers of sides

And numbers of angles on a

single side as time increases.

XXII

More often now

They come

The spells

not moving

not being able to move

not remembering

how to move

J. Michael Yates

then moving

like one who has never

before moved

all awkwardly

self-consciously

 the rage,

rage because rage

is the lifeline

the breakwater

against the undertow

of sadness

in which drowning

becomes possibility

crushed under certainty.

HONGYUN

XXIII

Between dawn and dusk

The only serious

philosophical question

is whether love can be

caused to go a distance

if not the distance

Between dusk and dark

comfortable elongated

vague

and hope that death

is final

And did one break the

laws of man and nature

with any style ?

XXIV

Shut up

You are only dead

Let me speak to you of real trouble.

J. Michael Yates

XXV

After I finished fearing

I might fall

Away and deep

Into the empty of sky,

I arose from my fearing place,

Of empty alpine swale

And pursued the moon:

Far below me,

It sounded and surfaced and sounded,

Through the cloud—corrugated

Midnight

Like a doomed, luminescent

Whale

HONGYUN

The rope of dread

Fast about my neck,

I followed,

As mind, alive,

Follows the body,

Long since dead.

The high clearing returns,

As does the noon.

In the heart of another part

Of sky,

A harpoon—barb of quarter—moon.

The fear falters, then subsides.

I am again alone.

The landscape blazes into phase

With light

None its own.

J. Michael Yates

XXVI

One day the parasite is

Simply there.

One day—sometimes the very

same day—the host is

simply gone.

XXVII

This is the truth.

This is the curtain.

It conceals the inner world.

Behind this curtain

There is nothing whatsoever to be seen.

The urge to go behind it

And verify is necessary.

For one or two.

Once behind it the thing that sees

Becomes something behind it to be seen.

HONGYUN

Behind the curtain

Becomes before it.

This is the truth.

This is the curtain.

It conceals the world outside entire.

XXVIII

At the end of hope,

Like the end of land,

Is the place to bog

And live where is nowhere

As nothing

Or become opposite,

Die andre Seite,

Of hope,

Of time,

J. Michael Yates

The other side of

Whatever it was

One needed

When he could remember.

XXIX

Forgive me,

Everyone

For I have done

Everything

And repented

Nothing

Including

Now

XXX

I had been trying to discover

The frontier

Between

What is clearly

Me

And what is clearly

The rest

Of

It all.

J. Michael Yates

BURN TISSUE CYCLE

I

A long green laze

Low over the windless, blue pools of days.

All the pater-noster ponds

Downpour toward the silt-fans of an imperious delta.

The red whales are not on fire. Sunset.

Or a coloured filter between the light and the world.

Moon-fangled dolphins crescent toward

The centre of the sea where light is still

A black vacuole.

II

The men going as far north as they can go,

Some pursued, some in pursuit,

Will pay little attention.

The north waits to burn

And they will poke the small lanterns

Of their two certainties

Into the moving corners of the northern dark.

But the days littered with black minutes have begun.

The skull is an interruption of breeze.

HONGYUN

Behind the eyes, ashes sift into soft dunes.

Blood the hound-figured

Holocaust.

III

The trees of heaven

And the trees or corporeity

Burn inequally.

The trees of hell: nonflammable.

Satiety is a small uncharted isle

In the orange open ocean of the hunger.

My time is of the old trees:

Dangerous, unstable, combusts

Quickly near others.

IV

Any scientist will tell you

Things burn best in the mist.

The fish which light the sea

At night are not mere phosphor turning,

And the water is not boiling

When the stream-green goes red with fins and flames.

J. Michael Yates

Call it oxidation, disarm it, call it rot,

But explain slowly, clearly, and decisively

To yourself

That this is the organic, the cycle, perfection.

And the oily ashes

Of the fish will save you.

V

A large fire at the centre.

Weak fires around the circumference where darkness ends

And skin begins.

From here where the scorpion self-struck,

To log to log, following the air,

Things burn on in toward the hotter hub,

Toward the place

Where, possibly, the light lives.

But the centre

Is too everywhere and too, too however.

There are at least two choices:

To peer into or pass through the mirror of ashes.

HONGYUN

VI

The embering logs of the vanished

Give the disfigured slopes of what is to come.

There might have been walls, at least,

And a roof between us and the rain.

Nothing came to hand

But the burning.

No name for what passed here. We left only frames of

Windows and doors too open

Upon the precincts where how to forget grew

And the stunted saplings

Of perhaps later are beginning to appear.

We turn, with the last droplets of fuel

Away and away to what might have been possible

Otherwise.

VII

I burned up my space

In a beach fire which warmed no one.

At the marge of the dark/light,

There was no voice drunkenly singing.

Once I mistook the clench of flames

J. Michael Yates

For something other: a distant harmonica,

Perhaps white foam on black rock burning dry.

The fear of being misunderstood: It burns well.

The fear of being understood burns better.

There are ten billion burning cells

On each side of the burning brain,

Each cell with as many as ten thousand burning endings.

For the fear of being ignored

I can neither ignite nor extinguish.

A day is a high pile

Of breaker-beaten wood

Dry, waiting for high hazard ...

Or lightning.

VIII

Sleep until it's alright.

The idea, for no reason, begins to burn.

Sleep or flame inhales

All the pilings of all possible wharves.

One awakens from one dream to another

Like ascending a burning building storey by storey.

The four corners of sleep

HONGYUN

Heat and curl until the daylight drops

And smoke goes the colours of darkness.

All the cargo craft will come aground

Or anchor out too far

Until the flames strangle, only the orange edges remain

And the squeak of substance giving.

IX

In a city of masts and fumes

I observe a man ablaze in a crowd whose edges I cannot see.

Those near him catch fire, head first,

Bend, twist, blacken

Then go out.

J. Michael Yates

AUTOMOBILE ACCIDENT

Like this she should have gone:

Like arias of sirens whirling,

Like crimsons on ebony whirling.

In the out-there she walks,

Beyond the tin clashing

Machine-flash of the living.

Beneath this huge obsidion,

She flows, her folds swishing

Over the curves of breathing.

This was a velvet mountain:

Outside it, a horn droning ...

An eyelid within, fluttering.

HONGYUN

NOTHING TROJAN NOR GREEK

A single sinew

Twitching within

A huge solitary beast.

Voice of a priest

From the coils

Of a writhing sea.

After this serpentine battle,

To go, loosed, sore-footed,

In the dry white alkaline fields.

J. Michael Yates

ONE HIEROGLYPH

The spirality of this:

Dark saint

In a dark land:

Dark finger toward a dark time.

First the swarming drone from the mountains.

Then the jagged line against the clouds.

Then our clothes and eyes and ears full of antennae and wings.

When his huge body

Takes him into its arms

I listen for the voices.

Later, the long skeleton

Lies shedding his flesh and the hot white

Circle expands. My eyes ambush my ears.

HONGYUN

THE CAVERN

Where some unenvisaged things

Have vanished,

There is no passage.

Through my hollowest center

Streams the subterranean river,

Deeper, and more silver

Than clearest remembrance

Of height in air.

Around me the albino fish

Who lost long ago

The need for eyes and eyes.

In the cool stone hallways,

The float into inlet into inlet

Into pool receiving pool ...

The quiet is coming.

And the dark.

J. Michael Yates

The river,

I know, is flowing close,

I know and know eddying close

To certain darker of the walls.

Somewhere distant a drop is falling

From a pool high on the cool ceiling.

Rings widening on the surface of a pool

Pass through me and through

The stone membranes of these

Walls and walls of walls.

A drop has fallen.

The river knows.

The river is all rings like this.

It flows and silently flows.

HONGYUN

Far darker now

Gone are the waving stone columns,

Continuing pillars in this temple of the dead

But I sense them passing,

Eyesneedle, needleeye, through I thread

Like the river - never touching—

As it wall after wall inside me threads.

When will I go with the blind white fish

In search of an absence of eyes?

The only vision is in clear black light

That rings the flow of a flowing night.

Only then will the colors come

Which wait within my walls.

J. Michael Yates

ICE CARNIVAL

Ice carnival

Is a mind's last festival

Before the run of a deadly spring.

This angular appurtenance,

Sharp, diffractive in blue winter light:

Blue ice sky, the green ice trees

Are of the mind's symbol-loving soul.

But pretend permanence ... for carnival.

I speak only of frozen figurations.

They impress, finally, the skyline of my life.

The river under me is moving,

I hear it rising as I carve the ice.

Steady the temperature, cold clear sight,

Nothing is north of a northern wish.

Time-floes dissolve in the river.

Who can breathe there but the fish?

HONGYUN

Think of a death by sunlight?

That slow swift stiffening at dark?

There an ice cosmos begins,

Here an ice idea leaves off.

Giddy the crystal music,

Giddy the pivotal dance on skates,

Sun on the ice goes deep in the eyes,

The river rising flows and waits.

Colours changing toward the nameless white,

Melting lines which join and join;

Close upon the river, the hot light.

J. Michael Yates

FERNWEH

The wind began

And hackles

Of the land

Arose on end.

Spannung between

Being seer, and,

At once, all

A seer has seen.

Late realization that

The history of one man

Is recorded always in

Unhurried loops of a woman's hand.

A white wind

Is moving in

The green thighs

Of the grain.

HONGYUN

There is music

I shall never

Play

Again.

J. Michael Yates

ONE AFTERNESS OF WAR

The war returns to Him this evening.

One green bombburst

On one horizon of one heart.

Tragicomic, the crows come

Like death,

Voluble, full of prank and posture.

With them, tragicomic life comes

Robber, scavenger,

Of high grace, swift of wing.

Born with love of whiskers,

Love of dirt and gunfire,

Still it took a man to kill a man.

We are alive red around the nostrils,

Breathe the blood-fumes of the battered air.

Men know this.

HONGYUN

The mind of the man plowing

Rustles like crenoline.

Earth is no flesh.

Women know this.

A great warrior is a saint:

His hand is the black hand of a half-god.

Chaplains know this.

He has crept inside a bombshell.

He dices there with soldiers and with clergy.

His son knows this, this evening. And the crows.

J. Michael Yates

GLASS AMOEBA

Within this bubble which begins

slowly, but clearly, to drift away

in a dimension perpendicular to

the line of time:

Earlier, time, for some of me,

had been severed by a guillotine

of glass. Behind the crystal

stricture, I observed the

continuum, without me, continuing,

its endless apollonian train.

The pane beneath me is double-strength

against the emptiness outside. Not

as cold as the lighted lens above —

microscope or moon.

HONGYUN

AIR MOVING

I like a breeze always,

Moving or a move-illusion always—

Even the even air-buffet

From a fan far away ...

The air stumbling and streaming

A fixed cylinder through the room.

Summers, I dream a current

Of women who understand

That illusory moving within

An ancient still-stand.

J. Michael Yates

HUNT IN AN UNMAPPED INTERIOR

I

A madman lost

In wilderness

And the bear everywhere:

Mind stalking mind,

Rooting through the

Refuse of a life,

The stricken thought

That doubles back in ambush.

II

Cold game trails

(forking paths which end and end)

Take him no human place.

Footing in deep muskeg

Is wet and unsteady.

III

Face for a

Dark winter, oncoming,

And a dark winter

Behind the face, gathering.

IV

Lean sheep

Pause now

On the higher

And higher crags.

V

The bear

Will not sleep

This winter.

J. Michael Yates

VI

What is it?

Instinct? We leave to starve

And double back this tangled way

To learn we left them

To become these skeletons?

VII

His madness

Was less simple hope

Than mammoth expectation.

HONGYUN

APPROACH

One deep fish

Flying moveless

Against the change

Of water ...

Reminds me

I haven't been alone

For a long time,

Perhaps ever.

Mind,

Is that it?

The only of

My creations

I can bear

To be

Alone with,

Silent?

J. Michael Yates

I cannot

Be ... alone ...

Who have

Nothing for

Myself ... in

Silence.

Shadow

Of my hand

Passing over

Water:

Claw,

Wing,

What has been

Alone,

Ever,

In empty

Water?

HONGYUN

SENTRY

I patrol my

Small, shrinking

Wilderness. An

Imbecile duty.

Nothing out there

In the bleak,

In the blaze,

Threatens. Yet

Vines, the trees

Methodically go.

Perhaps

While I sleep.

Still I break, often,

From the growth,

Bellowing to stun

What kills a wilderness.

J. Michael Yates

How to destroy

What has no

Knowledge of itself.

Before this Is ...

An axe, I shall

Turn toward these

Strange last trees,

These changing vines.

HONGYUN

ONE IMMOBILE NOON

In motion, only,

A bird, shot,

Falling — or a man

With shredded wings

Toward the sea.

J. Michael Yates

EMERGENCE OF AN EYE

At a swirl

On the dark surface,

I have a fish.

I didn't wish

To lure anything.

Length starved

Slim as a snake,

It lies

In the grass,

Still, resisting

With one sunken eye.

HONGYUN

In the dark mirror

Within the skull-shore,

Something too familiar

Begins to form.

At a sheer edge,

I release the freak

Without a noise,

Without a ripple,

Almost.

J. Michael Yates

DEATH OF A FISH

Death of a fish

Is drying of the film

Which actuates all senses.

Things don't

Go at once,

Fisherman,

Stiff here and glaring

Too many moments

Inside the shell,

This darkening object

In bright grass

Beside surging water.

HONGYUN

LOCUST SPRING

One by one

The heavy doors

Of my senses

Swing open into the spring.

Things I spent the winter naming

Struggle free of

Their round syllables,

Fly into the fruit trees,

Sing down the full throats

Of the fattening birds.

In the dark

When the air relaxes

The rages of singing and wings,

Small circles descend

Toward the grass:

Each encapsulates seventeen years.

J. Michael Yates

EARLY SUMMER

Half-crazed by virginity

And the hot, swollen air,

Summer women swarm the season.

The feeling buzzes, quiets,

Held between slim fingers

By its translucent wings.

That stroll of theirs is the changeless thing:

Covering with cautious steps the thin, brilliant skins

Of fruit until the deep seeds inside blacken and wrinkle.

My heavy body, damp, listless,

Falls upon my mind, and things suffocate

One after one in this dark, airless room.

HONGYUN

THE SEASONAL

The blood of things

Braces against the dark air and delivers:

Too many and too quick.

To lick these many muzzles

There are never

Tongues enough.

Where the licking must begin ...

At the still form of a first-born?

At the squirming uncertainty of a last?

That the eyes of the sub-animal

Are yet not open,

Puts the question.

J. Michael Yates

Below the collar of light

Gathers the thunder-signal,

The tooth of time

At the base of the skull:

The vixen protecting her pups with death.

Calm reswallowing storm.

HONGYUN

ARACHNID

Ideas circle so sluggishly.

A tentacle of autumn must be

Uncoiling deep in the clouds.

One alights ... barely struggles

Half-strangled in my filaments of words.

Soon it blinks stupidly, surprised.

After formalities, the silent buzz,

It hangs thereafter, lifting a little in breeze:

Transparent thorax, a bit of brittle wing.

J. Michael Yates

THIRD EYE

Against dark angry circles

Of earlier, impatient form,

The high white skies inside whiten.

The clear eye soared,

Cocked and glared,

Awaited the shadow.

When the rain-season ceased

And sand-dolphins foundered over the land,

The sage and cactus concealed, after all,

No new mammal nor bird. A few

Still point toward the circles and speak:

These vanished angles of an angry eye.

HONGYUN

AFTER

After the earthquake,

The wave was certain.

And certain to leave the double city

Dead or deeply changed.

We say Yes the water

Came over us, although

Structures, streets, the old

Gestures all remain.

We live in peril of nothing now

On earth of infinite afternoon.

J. Michael Yates

A MATHEMATICS

The beast at the fringe

Of the limitless herd

Pauses for return

Of hunger, only.

Slaughter goes

To my sick and my slow

For preserving their long maladies.

The dead feed the earth

And the earth will

The inevitable.

Come treachery of season,

Come betrayal of pelt

Or foliage, this dark winter,

Even the defenseless shall survive:

Their bitter inedible numbers....

HONGYUN

WHEN WOLVES

When wolves,

When black-burnished wolves

With their moon-green eyes,

Turn suspicious of stupid prey,

Wolves turn their icy eyes upon themselves.

All autumn

I watched the heavy bulls, single, slow,

Rise along blue peaks toward snow,

Then descend into the storm-centres

Of their merest blood.

My mind turned

As the moose turned,

Fur, feathers,

Weather,

And the leaves.

J. Michael Yates

Beneath the pale-green

Snake fire that strikes and straightens

Across the wide winter night,

My eyes turn to yours, my eyes,

Your moon-coloured eyes.

HONGYUN

WAY INTO WINTER

One final mouth of water

Speaks from its dark center

In the freezing lake.

No birds circle now

But in the orange-rose skies

Behind my eyes: large black birds.

I've been to the fire

At the center of the earth:

My steps shall not snow-over before spring.

J. Michael Yates

TRANSPARENCY OF BLACKNESS

1

If there is nothing,

I know, still, an animal is swimming

Toward me through dark water,

Through wet darkness

Without sense

Of malice

Or of kill.

2

The humour of a wilderness:

These too-many waiting

Ways to die.

And none of them

The ways men wait to die.

3

One wants his own way,

His own last hour,

His own last syllable,

His face.

HONGYUN

4

Outside me,

There's machinery,

The mathematics one

Loses one within.

5

And here, something rising

From a surface

Two wet soundless

Forepaws on a beach.

J. Michael Yates

DOCTRINE

There is some chance, when I arise,

The landscape will arise with me and follow

Or I have never been wherever I have been.

One wounded caribou

May cross again and make

Yet the crossing of another year.

There is some chance a young bull moose

Will go exiled, warped head-piece, emasculated

By wolves at practice, in wait for another hunger.

Warmth waits in the deepest snow

When the dogs ignore a mammoth moon

And the plume of the semi-volcano rises cold.

Gods and winters give, but first, receive.

Now it is short low sunset between two huge nights.

I live where a wolf turns when there is no game.

HONGYUN

HUNTER

The animals approach too near now.

A final hunter sheds his human scent.

I wish sometimes I might have wished

To walk upwind all of my days.

J. Michael Yates

PRELUDE

Black trees on the shore

Of the sky.

Behind them,

A quiet lightning, winking.

White roots, fork

After fork, divide

My dark earth.

It's trouble overhead,

And here I am, whatever,

Armed with the mandible of a beetle.

HONGYUN

WHALE

When the darkness appears just a little darker

Than it should, go liquid, it is only

The whale rising. The biggest beast is not

Unexpected; the instant of arrival is surprising.

Go liquid. Get darker than the dark,

When, unexpectedly, the largest darkness

Is rising darker than all darkness should,

The ice floe is breaking up instead

Of merely melting. Swallow the water.

The whale is smaller than water. Swallow.

J. Michael Yates

GOOD TO SAY

I think it might be good to say:

Nothing moves in mysterious ways

Although some are occasionally curious.

Courage, we know, occasionally flags just for a moment.

Odds — it makes sense — are that cowardice does too.

Perhaps one might be able to slip through the chink and get it.

The Me has even less substance

Than the I, and everything I do waves

Goodbye, Yates, goodbye, goodbye.

HONGYUN

DRIVING

I must remain close to myself in these times.

Stay, space, at a distance. I prefer going

Down a long darker valley between mountains

Whose slopes are fatigued with avalanches

To even a single view of a desert or a prairie.

Unlike time, space is dangerous.

Time, for all its costumes, can only run out.

But before and after, space abides.

Light is the supreme language, conversing with itself

Just beyond the ridge where the rim rider rides.

You must cup space in your hands and then

Blow it away. Perhaps space will notice.

Perhaps hands cannot hold a vacuum.

The dog in me suspects that space does not care

What it contains, whether vacuum, whether air.

J. Michael Yates

I must keep space at a remove a little longer.

It will come for me in its own black time.

I prefer rotten insides and an avenging face.

I've driven a jinxed car through a fixed race.

HONGYUN

EVENT HORIZON VERNAL

When the dewdrop door yawns, do not enter.

Regardless how vividly you feign the colours

Of the fighting fish, the door will close behind,

And your gills will not come back to you.

J. Michael Yates

THERE WILL BE NO MORE PASSENGERS

There will be no more passengers

Traveling great distances

To embrace me at the terminal.

I shall not voyage to their places

Because I have no further messages

And have grown too bored to make lies.

Hopefully their faces are gone from me.

Texture of legs is helpfully volatile.

Some limbs have grown shorter or longer than they were.

Nothing undergirds the ways between one life and another.

Just behind what is known of all police lies

What is known of all criminals. Et au verso.

Having taken a wrong turning, a man was struck blind,

En route to a city which existed only in what is called mind.

A journey whose object was to destroy what he later became.

HONGYUN

Another built

World's most misguided ship

At the behest of a delusion.

One sat outside an imaginary wall

And cursed a perverse god

For killing a plant which was not growing between his feet.

The escalators descend always up with their

Streams of graduated burden. The riders look up and up.

None notices the escalators ascending down even faster.

There will be no more passengers

Traveling great distances to embrace me at the terminal.

I am not there to greet them, and the places to arrive are gone.

J. Michael Yates

THIRTEEN

When the blind bulls of light

Craze down the valley wall,

Divide the half-darkness into wedges.

Small lives begin inside the transparent hedges;

There has been no noise at all.

Electricity falters between wrong and right.

Who has never seen the silver eyes

Between the moving lids of fern

Has been spared.

More than one has dared

Look but dared never learn;

Never question how a night sky dies.

Rose evening tangled in the velvet horns,

A stag rises through the dusk-dark hay.

The last of the parachutes come collapsing down.

HONGYUN

Nothing further escapes the black ground.

An end was visible, there was no way;

Space surged in where time was torn.

Darkness, too, was a sieve

Gray, gray as the other part:

The powerline is broken.

Light goes token

As language against the dark

Between past and future. Nothing gives.

J. Michael Yates

ISOTHERM THIRTY-SIX

If you glimpse my body-heat

Gliding like a blue-eyed white tiger

Among the umber and light

Of the glaciers and moraines,

Shoot, please, to kill.

I've grown too slow to recapture.

Without heat I cannot do. Only be.

But without me, without name,

My heat will die a long and painful flame.

THE KNOWING

The dark owls roosting in the yellow acacia
Today everything is a sign for something else.

I am never too old to be
Guilty of being too innocent.

Sea lions among the herring
Off the point.

The in-drawn bark comes
Through my half-consciousness
Like a round of black ending
Through the glittering bits of swarming time.

Too soon things which have not shown their faces
Show their teeth.

J. Michael Yates

SIGN

Something wishes just to be what it is.

One comes to regard time as nonexistent hazily.

You have something to fall back on.

You do that: Fall back.

One year was like every other.

Eventually everything would happen.

Nothing can be just what it is.

HONGYUN

CEDAR WAXWING

This is the centre

The place where the dust

Cannot enter

Neither can the dust

Which thickens on everything inside

Get out

J. Michael Yates

PHOENIX

Not only can I not have the Phoenix without the ashes,

I cannot have the Phoenix without the fire.

HONGYUN

SAPSUCKER

All night I lay not listening to the cougar calling through black rain
and mist white in the puncturing light

The sound fell into the seam between a child crying out in the night
and the mew of a small bird of charcoal and crimson

The auditory cougar occupied my silence as ferns occupy the fragile
space between strong trees—not sunspokes—, variegated green and
all the fall of shadow into blinding black. Not that, but that inexactly

Lupin and foxglove and skunk-cabbage were part of the cougarnight,
but not part of my not listening

The child life of the cougar cry gives me disquiet but not panic nor
knowledge. I speak more to the small black and red bird with the
unpleasant name

I have come to contain this mountain, the mist-space it creates
surrounding

Each day spring breaks again, each day a little higher, as the skirts of
snow rise

Tonight in the rainy cougar, all seasons interwoven on this mountain
and contained

Tonight I am alone in this place

Only what I say of this remains

J. Michael Yates

SPARROW

The insects are up: the wind is down. There are the parts which remain aloft only in stillness and beneath the weight of shadow, and then the parts which fly in high wind in wide space and full in the sun in its own proper place.

These are separate currents of knowing which should not and confluence under the skin.

Hawk and hummingbird share one and different air.

Between the gods I curse in the dark and the stone over which I stumble in the dark, a war moves along a jagged path.

Intermittent bolts of peace startle more than ease. I have been too long enclenched with it all.

Come sleep, come death, come release.

HONGYUN

THE FLUME—YUN CYCLE I

The flowing of us:

The strong weathering flume

Which transports the sound of you

To me in a farther room

J. Michael Yates

THE TIME—YUN CYCLE II

The time is come

You are the one

Who has been moving

Toward me

All our lifetimes long.

For us, time is perpetual now

And it seems most magnificent how

Well we use it to meld.

Beauty, almost unbearable beauty

Is your tawn skin

Easing up toward mine

And shining close

As I ease in

HONGYUN

PREHISTORIC MEALS

Faith like an eagle blinded

In the brimstone miasma

Which hangs between the mill and the sun.

Malaxation of all memorious:

Faith blinded by the fire-tempered cudgel

In the cave.

Overwhelm the outrageous sheep.

Cling to the deep wool of the elsewhere

And ride, rider, ride.

The reasons for moving,

The reasons for remaining still break

Like cheap fishing rods at real contact.

Lurch slightly

Between this and that.

It becomes itinerary.

J. Michael Yates

Sooner or later a new island

Older than consciousness.

The mist is not lifting, no.

HONGYUN

THE MOST INTELLIGENT CEPHALOPOD

In a fury of ink

And chilly colour change,

The small octopus jetted into me.

Then grew.

What it fed upon, I never knew

Until far too late.

It takes me to wait beneath rocks in pools

Between the go and go of world.

J. Michael Yates

FROM THE GREAT BEAR LAKE MEDITATIONS

The wolves say to the dogs what the madman of me says to the citizen. I need to go fishing until I need to return.

The fish move with the winds, their sails under the currents under the winds. A figure sails tracery of the darker, narrower peninsulas: warped fingers of a mad continent trailing in stagnant water beneath the dark. I steer gnarled beside myself as it struggles in dreams. Moss in the meshes and the mad tangles of a tree heaving through higher and higher swells. Silt stirs up through all the clear water - stains the cups of the tottering crests shattering through the delta flats. Soon now. Be quiet. Breathe.

The totem poles are turned toward the river. Beneath these the cleared land is pinned like a drying skin. The colour green is treacherous. The headstones are turned toward the peaks.

First sense as I awaken under the fans of northern summer light: perhaps I shall get well here. Who can remain that long? Light has more duration than the eye. To remain too long is to become a sickness of another syndrome. I've summoned and survived that too - and carry it, asleep now, in the caves and crevasses of my blood.

I awaken in a rage, with the exhaust of bitter warfare trailing through my skull just behind eyes and tongue. Something or someone has been feeding on me in my sleep. Or worse: nothing has been feeding on me in my sleep. Only these fumes, and sense of a violence just ceased in the interior sky. I can't lie awake and wait for it ... perhaps:

make a raft of consciousness and float it north down the Mackenzie River of sleep. I'll observe and observe and observe while whatever it is that eats me, eats me. I become this single appetite.

I persist in a little fabric between me and the world. This is the sleep inside a tent on an airless, sunstung afternoon. The sleep beyond mosquitoes and black flies that close in and in upon the beast that ceases to stir. This is the orange sleep that seeps and clings like mire. The muskeg and the clear streams are going away. The wet sleep comes for me like water on the rise. Snow-caps in the distance are burning. Somewhere in the extinguishing light, the plume of a crowning forest fire. Whatever will enter this canvas crypt can have me. Nothing comes, and I can't rise. The tick of a clock somewhere beneath things diminishes with the last fly that circles outside like a plane coming to rescue the lost in sleep. The mouth of flat blackness is closing. Sleep stiffens through me to the bayous beyond dream. I shall die here in this uncertain growth. Seams of the tent will give, canvas and skin will sink beneath the ash of the fire that has been burning toward me forever. The wind changes. The fire goes green. This is the sleep of mastadons and mammoths, not the sleep of winter bears I've buried beneath cornices of words. On the surface of the tar-pit, stillness over the blackness signals the stop of a monstrous metabolism. The undergrowth is zombied in the thin stutter of heat. The coming destruction. The roads I followed here are washing away. This is the Lazarus who returned with no more to show than a yawn, the taste of dying in his mouth, vague hunger, thirst and no recollection of awakening at an earlier dawn. This was the sleep within the tent that I sewed. I entered, shut out the weather and went to sleep for darkness' sake. The afternoon and the insects have waited. I dream I only dream I am awake.

Legend: The God in the sun made two men. In the hands of one he placed a book. An axe he handed the other. *Decree*: In search of one another they shall circle the earth forever. *Curse:* May you walk upwind all of your days. *Act:* The left hand loses memory of the right.

J. Michael Yates

Neither blade nor word gives the feel of gods at this long high noon of the night. The wind, like consciousness, appears only in other things.

☯

How long ago is it that my ancestors kept slaves? What remains of their blood in my veins? And is it possible to care about such things? Then, they bought men by the lifetime; this indian is mine by the week, my guide. Things have changed: if he were white, the price would be the same.

☯

At least two rivers confluence inside me: one clear. The substance between them is giving up everything. *It is the strange habit of the people in this locale to burn the home of one who has experienced tragedy. Sometimes, because of its proximity, or because it belonged to the victim, a totem pole is burned. In 1936, a flood, literally hundreds of totem poles were lost.* I'm moving to higher and higher ground. The turns of earth and air remain.

☯

Say the word. *Skeena.* Say the words. *Skeena, Kispiox, Stikeen, Babine.* What sounds are these? *The long e's, the words of water, the terror of moving, silence sheathes the current, the long e's veil the faces of a fisherman's mysteries.* Mists moving over the faces of the river. *The river bears itself away in mist.* Say the invisible fish. *The fishermen with nets have forgotten the fish.* The fish. *Even the fishermen who wait like the bear at the turn of the water, even the fishermen who draw their nets through the darkening water, the fishermen are uncertain.* And therefore wait. *The fisherman who no longer wonders doesn't put his nets in the morning.* No one gathers in the dusk to see what the light has given up to mesh. *The fisherman who no longer wonders no longer sees the light change upon the changing water.* The fisherman no longer wishes for *something strange from familiar water, something foreign from familiar water, something familiar from foreign water.* The fisherman no longer wishes *a use for this being alive.*

128

HONGYUN

☯

This is no ordinary piece of stone. In the rising firelight, it was taken in the hands of a great chief and brought down upon the head of another indian to kill him. Not in war, but celebration, was the "slave-killer" used. Unless giving and sacrifice can be considered aggression. Notice the excellent craftsmanship and simplicity of design. Only here and there it's been - from excessive handling, perhaps - worn smooth.

☯

Alcohol is what this village died of. When they made the pubs legal for *indians, they got in their boats and headed for the mainland, every one of them, right down to the last clootch and papoose.* A wind of silence blows across the point, broken only by the seething clouds of black flies which rise out of our steps in the deep grass. *Or religion. Maybe they were dying of religion anyway. Look at that church.* The church, the broad-axed cabins, and the smokehouses have weathered well. But the grass and weeds are pulling this clearing back into the bush. *They left everything—haying equipment, tools, horses, dogs, nets, boats— everything they couldn't take in one trip. Nobody much has been here in ten or fifteen years.* In the chartreuse light between two cabins, a fat white horse stares at us, undecided, then gallops up the mountain through the high growth of the hay-fields towards the pines. *A man could make a good ski-resort on that slope, with a little backing. But it's reservation; even though they don't live here anymore, it's still reservation land. Over there's the cemetery; the black flies would be even worse there.* We push off past the fossils of boats whose prows are just visible between waves.

☯

Soon. *The fire or the storm.* Might as well burn now. When the storm gets here, lightning'll ignite everything the heat doesn't burn. *No matter what: fire.* You can't run everyone out of the bush. *How do you tell a man to leave his home because he's in danger?* He is danger. *Water's coming up. You better pull out. They'll have you on the line, black in the face, shovel in your hand like the rest.* Fire now'll burn all summer. *They clean out the pubs first. Take everybody. Men. Nobody drinks in public when the fire hazard is high.* It's against the law not to fight the fire. You have to fight the fire. But they can't make you get into a plane. They can't make you get into a plane or a boat. One time I pulled that on 'em and took a week to walk in ten miles. Fire was out when I got there.

How far north will a mind consent? I'm alive because I wonder how far things can go. Anything that survives its original purpose becomes a record. Anything that survives. A grinning indian prepares my lunch at the shore.

A bright scream of heat goes up from the landscape. And then the fire-whispers between the fingers of the spruce. Electricity gathers in the polarized weather as it does at sixty below. Was it rain or sunlight I wished for? Death and madness quarrel over me. The sex of the moon is uncertain. The lake, perhaps, won't be there when I turn.

When am I? *Soon. Possibly. Consider the shape of the fountain. Enter the water, the foliage of water, the flora. In the spaces between strong currents, between the leaves of the giant ferns of water, lies the answer.* The water winds around it and posses to the sea. It is the rock. The answer. I am the answer. And it's moving. *It voyages. Only the water is fixed.* Consciousness desires.... *Consciousness is without desire. It is a thing—the no-thing—without desire or memory. Perfect consciousness has the memory of a stone. It contains its own everything.* Consciousness desires to fountain in the midst of flooding water. Consciousness wishes to bloom at the centre of present circumstance and arrange in the manner that mind arranges history. But here, in the hollow of the present, the centre, not at the edge, the crumbling bank, not at the shore where the bones of the fish are strewn. *Angels have no memory. Angels desire nothing.* The farthest risk is what I'm waiting for. *The great cedars of the rain-forest have skins of chartreuse moss. Their lives are indefinite because of this magnificent mould. The spaces between*

them are dim and green at the boundaries that never specifically begin. It rains always. Corpuscle by corpuscle I'm washing to the sea. *A man is almost all water. Spend some time with the slugs. Construct yourself of rain.* I don't want the sea, its acres, its gallons, its commandments, its minutes, its roman numerals, its logic — all the death a sea is made of. *The tides in your cells are busy at your sea-walls.*

Teeth of air close upon the teeth of water. Between circles a man in a small boat, trolling. One bird, one nothing lighter than another. The years-long fires under the tundra is what's left to understand -voluptuous craving and thin satiety. Language melts in my mouth like August ice caught in a flashchange of weather. Nouns dissolve in search for things to name, the search for nothing, the no-thing at the edges of wind and water. Sound of a loon stuns the distance, a bloom, a hatch of insects. The bird or something to do with birds follows me into my sleep. One particle of the dark I carry with me into the light. It's nothing I would name

There were some secrets I wished to conceal from the wilderness, but a wind detected whisky on my breath. The only motion was my distant hand which placed a bottle of Scotch on a rock between me and the water, fourteen hundred feet deep. Carefully I mixed alcohol, lake and me. In this manner, this north has come to be.

How shall I contain fourteen hundred feet of water — is there anything in the labyrinth of my shoals and bays that deep? Nothing can live at that depth that I know of. Only the nothing there in that final darkness survives. It is the nothing at the floors of all my black water that whispers into my dreams: I am alive.

I take today on a light line in fair weather: today, the fish-shape, between me and the bottomless water. The struggle is longer than

its hours. My fingers chill and cramp while the line cleaves round and round my small boat afloat upon a mirror. Although I shake the white knuckles of all my hands, a stone stillness fills the insides of my bones. The only significant thing — it seems to me — is this imbecile station against what I cannot see — to hold as if my line cannot break, as if darkness shall never fall again, as if the ice won't close about me if I stay. *It will be enough,* I say again, *if I can see it only once. Only see.* And my time comes round once again, great fins swirling slowly, half in water, half in air. The gill-bellows draw in and draw in what I can't name breath. I become a dangerous liaison between the water of my life and the air of my death. I pushed off from an old encampment, a forgotten place of will. There is nothing now but water and water won't stay still. The sky is larger than sky here, too much horizon, no possible shore. Now is as close as I have ever been, this now with its longer form and slimier sides. And now someone takes the gaff to drive something substantial into the mandible of my time. I whisper: *Pass cautiously ... don't touch my exhausted line.* It's impossible, with grace, to intervene; the small knot at the lure goes loose, and today rows slowly down the thermoclines of deepening green.

On this island too north for trees, I fish for arctic char. The ice-blue landscape is the colour of the ice-blue water. A small seal reclines and watches from a rock across the stream. I lie that only water passes between the beast and me.

❦

As I've made myself of alcohol, paper and computer circuitry, these eskimos have carved themselves from soapstone: simple, heavy line, surface so fragile it can be disfigured by a manicured fingernail. Now and then a seal surfaces inside them. Their minds are the lichen that takes these stone islands into its hands. Tethered to this passage of time as their starved curs are tethered to their stakes, they, like me, await nothing busily.

❦

I return here. Like a man who has bombed a city and returns as a tourist, I return here — a camera between me and the world. How to wrest my wilderness from the teeth of all my cannibal cities. One man of me goes ghostly through all the walls. He lives without substance and has only nothing to say. The rest live as animals at a zoo. And over-civilized men who gaze down the colours of an arctic lake. In the twilit negative landscape, a self-conscious nothing moves away: a pike which will die with a pike in its throat. Geographic and historic distances are coevals. I can fall up the terrible blue canyons between the clouds.

These peaks which mouth the air of the distance jut nowhere from nowhere. Bitten between fog and cloud. So long as there are peaks when I look up, I won't depress the trigger. But the days when the mist gauzes in around me; these I must treat instant by instant. I can almost wish for cold, its clarity. Except for the business with body: sustaining the small halo of heat that fills the vacuum between living and not living. It distracts. Perhaps total preoccupation with body constitutes ideal loss of body. I can't stand too much clarity, too much vision, that much cold. Or the real mountain is: changes of air and light, presence and absence of the seen. Or the real mountain is the one I fangle despite the overcast — one more clarity of which I can't stand too much.

The first aurora of my life. I've been with a woman and now this colour green comes for me. I can't rise. This savage light that stiffens then dissolves, absorbs my use. The wilderness wants everything. The wolves of green light are gathering by the river. On the other side a huge animal with antlers like two carved hands opened toward the sky is voyaging through the black air. The water: low and lowering. Each hour the cold deepens. A death of water is certain and soon, and I'm traveling north to bathe away this alien scent upon me.

That this town died of earthquake would be difficult to guess, arriving over the well-kept road by car. The cabins, the hotel, the general store still stand at the angles of their builders' intentions. The spaces between them are heavily overgrown. And some enemy of Plato has painted dancing ghosts on the weathered cabin-sides. The white of the ghosts is going transparent. Beside the doorway to the saloon, an enormous piece of raw metal rests on a wooden platform. A sign reads: *2400-lb. nugget of copper.* As my small plane lifts from a nearby lake to fly me to the fish, and threads its way up the steep river canyon, my pilot points below where three railway passenger-cars are rusting on a half-mile of track. Before and behind them, only craggy features of a cliff-face incised by the earthquake. Along that narrow ledge, the spine of a mining operation led to the sea, to a once-busy port which died as the feet die when the head has been destroyed.

Geese arise in my inside skies when the wolf-pack gathers in my groin. At the full mood of the moon, I listen with the ears of an animal. My body glows in the dark with nostalgia for something I can no longer conceive, and I begin to dream I have only dreamed large cities on other continents where my foreigness spoke to their women with the voice of a serpent. The difference between feeling and feeling about: empty containers draw me. High peaks draw me.

Something is rising in the black throat of the sky. Something draws me into the earth by my eyes. just beneath them the avalanches of flesh begin. The language of a man alone in the bush goes the colours of boulder-fields and lichen. Through the zodiacal light, he sees a bear the colour of ice waiting on the ice for something to surface for air. The memory in his fingertips begins to callous over. Or to freeze.

And now, only one dread: I'll die before I've said all my objections to living. I cannot say I want to live. But something in me, some part, wants to want to live. The days come away like cold-mauled rocks upon this beach. In my other place, I'd have said: like bricks from a ruined wall.

I'm here to remember my animal, that ghost-beast of many shapes —sometimes a solitary caribou, more often a bear. A man comes north to become an animal, to turn the whole day toward food and a place to sleep warm. Small cracks begin at the bases of marble angels that were his ideas. His days come down like trees felled to feed an insatiable fire. Like trees felled to raise a cabin whose windows and doors vanish a little hour to hour.

Each hour I deposit another stone in the pack-sack beneath which Adam staggers. The stones have faces and scientific names. Their voices are the colours of moss and breaking. It's the ivory of Adam's bones that the Eskimos carve. Configurations of his face appear upon the water between swells where Time was the whale who swallowed Adam, then made for the cold waters of the north. All the Eves of my history are sleeping beneath warm darkness somewhere near the Equator. Their shapes are those of continents secure on maps of explored terrain. The motion of water is mine, and intermittent glimpses of illusory isles. Daily they sleep farther from me. Daily the dark arrives sooner.

Noah wasn't the first sad craft of stunned, delivered, bitching animals, but fool enough not to be the last. I leave myself running through this blackest rain toward the helm and, instead, join the unbuoyant odd numbers. One man with the whole of perpetuity bellowing in his hold. The rain ceases, it was said. No wind at noon-blue of the moon. Over the gunwale one of us slips continually. All afternoon we sprawl in the shade of the olives beneath the gloomy mating of the doves — grinning, nudging, shouting when the crude boat again blunders by.

Beyond the wall of the boundless city, I seat myself. On a stone. To wait. Whales of the night air pass over me and beneath themselves, blowing jets of darkness into the dark. The long leaves of my madness spangle still with droplets of light.

The opaque man closes doors carefully between rooms. Now. There is no humour left in the transparent man's passing through. Between them the old inquiries have become unaskable as unanswerable. One no longer longs to dissolve into a northern landscape. Nor one to do something about the tides. The clams at low water, birds walking overhead. Vessels inside the dark, their hives of light moving over almost all water. Winter to winter when the aurora goes mad green, they ease their rockers, peer across these surfaces, then resume.

Always, before I've seen the wolf, the wolf has seen me twice. The green wolf at the end of the world takes me between his teeth: the bird caught in the thicket of its own camouflage. The fire-wolf is the ravenous realist. Intelligence, my portly prey, is the farthest fathom of hunger. When the wind-wolf curls about the cold trunks of the trees, the legs of the chairs quake in all my rooms and outside an eagle falls upon a fish I've spawned all morning. Time storms the spaces between things. I stuff the hours with syllables and give them plastic eyes. I've given over to the ice-wolf, that we might melt together and the edges of the landscape soften. The earth-wolf waits for me at the centre of open tundra. On the convex of her eye, all my possibility turns. And the dog-pups voyage around the fixed gigantic bitch - the black of their antics, the gray of her gigantic waiting.

I'm coming soon to the end of me, to the edge, the drop-off, to the place where the tundra halts, even the mosses don't survive, and the ice presides for all seasons. The auditory landscape thins and my ears are going blind of silence. I'll strike through, Then drown in the clear cold water at the bottom of the fall. And try to know I'm drowning as

I drown. I came up from the south, from the equator at the centre of all bone where the hot dark whispered into my animal listening. But there was something else, always something else, had to be, and I'm moving out from the hollows of the tree-root places into the gaining light, over the thunderous boulders of the river-bed which shatter one another in high water, I pierce the thickets of nerve at the bone and enter the hazy skies of flesh, the skies the colour of lichen on the deadfalls, pass the ligaments, wade the currents of muscle, then wait days, often, for the water to drop in the glacial braids, to prepare for a crossing. The mad arctic light of the outside finally finds me through the crusted snows of my skin. I'm coming soon to the end of me, to the membrane which contains all my mortal remains. The needle of my compass points always north like the finger of a prophet until I become north, and, like a shot swan, it bewilders in terrible circles. There is no object in the white landscape upon which to triangulate. Hunter and weapon merge, and the quarry whirls at the box-canyon wall to battle the nothing at all behind him.

A gloomy peace. Pause between what nothing explains and everyone understands. Files I'll never open ever again, now, the leaded-glass doors, the stained-glass lampshades and windows. Where it's been, more or less, and its names, I've known always. Quietly. Now - still in silence - exactly. On the tundra I watch a grizzly stalk a black bear stalking a squirrel.

The tse-tse fly the man seeks through the streets of dreamed and dreamless sleep alights upon the forearm of the dream and bites -almost — before the man awakes. He dreams a man marooned in the long late August light. The droves of dying flies become aircraft always about to appear over the horizons of coma. When a plane passes over his bedroom, he looks toward the ceiling for a fly. Tanganyika, the arctic and several cities fuse on the bulb of his multiple eye. An insect is flying toward him in the darkness, an insect flying blind. A suicide, the man seeks, a death outside himself, yet inside his command: centrifugal sleep, the man seeks, for a centripetal man.

Empty powerlines walk on stilts over my ridges. Empty causeways walk over my water. A farm: one animal standing out its life within fences. Only I and the mountain aren't between the mountain and me.

And so the barbarians came. Over the high walls of my skull, they dropped like water over a broken dike. How easily they overpowered my fortifications disappoints me. Now they mingle, at the centre of my head, bewildered. They came to conquer - in the grand manner — but there was nothing, really, nothing at all to oppose ... but one another, and all are deeply weary from the journey. Little by little, selection occurs. I notice then some wear less hair than before. As though taken by gradual and beneficent contagion, knot after knot of pillagers and rapists begin to civilize, build walls and wait through the long-voweled afternoons for the arrival of danger from the north.

The still dark figures in a line against the white mountain are still climbing. The picks in their hands are light. The pianos on their backs are heavy. The other side of the pass, beyond the permafrost edges of the photograph, the whores pare their fingernails and wait.

The hands in my head were fumbling, fumbling with some last something when the Judas goat appeared upon the hillcrest against the rising moon. A madman sank through the herd, palms turned toward the light: *I'm the war: I Am the War.* The two fish his hands were vanished across night the seafloor. Moondown swam with the madman under the surface of the earth. No hands molested the twitching animals. Smokestains of bomb-bursts began again over the curve of the hill. We would again wait. The goat arrives again.

Again for nothing. I surface again, move among you again, this time without a sound: two sharks rising toward your still shapes upon the ground.

I haven't time, because the glacier dwindles beneath this escalate light. If the ice has always been going, I haven't always known it, and there isn't — clearly — time. I sense the fish begin to rot before the boat casts off — so little has time been. The absence of anyone or anything by which I measure my motion outside time commits me to death before my death. In time, but not of time, the fish move not moving in the shapes of water that move and do not move. Ice is and is not, quite simply. Emptiness contains is emptiness contained. Nothing speaks for the blue moraines.

I am alive. Since the beginning. Long before the ice. The muskoxen do not run from me. In the tar-pits with the great reptiles I died. I sleep with the mastodons beneath the permafrost of Alaska. I am as extinct as all the extinct animals and as alive as those you see. Mud-volcanoes of the tundra disfigure me. All adaptations and mutations are within and without my body. I am white as winter ptarmigan, blue as glacial bears, black as black leopards of the black land. When I die, so will the world die with me. After the thaw, I appeared with these alluvial lines some call a face. My name is Nothing; I contain all time and all space.

I've been handled like a dangerous animal always. I'm a dangerous animal. More and more it grows dangerous carrying my life like a deadly weapon. Concealed: all six senses in ten mountains in two pockets of my coat.

In, inward deeper now, light dies into the dark. A blue-white ring beside you moves, moves as you move - but more precisely, then

J. Michael Yates

glows before you like an eye. Around you, it closes. Everywhere the
sight of ticking and the sound of light. Just beyond: the quiet and the
dark. Perhaps leave it on a rock...because you've been all it owned,
you cannot leave it there. Your senses, eager, unsatisfied, remember
numbers, light and noise. Drive your wrist against the stone — flesh
motionless and stunned — this shock-resistant thing of yours is more
in itself than you, alone. Three suspended fish of light swim within
an invisible dome. No magnetism of the walls silences the ticking of
an eye alone. Beneath the deepest lightless sea you're certain those
hands would continue around. Run down. Never as long as you live.
Alive, you move, and as you move, time winds and winds itself. Look
away, hold your ears, recollection sees the dials you've known: the
irreversible catacombs of minutes, hours, years. You tick together on
and on, immortal metal, mortal flesh. Nerves bristle out like gears.
Here brass and dendrite mesh.

☯

What points on the compass if all directions are equal, if all directions
are inaccessible, if there is no way there from here? No way out: No
way in.

☯

The faces of time are circular, the faces of space are circular—and I,
at the centre where watch and compass do not see. Time declares:
I am dying. Space declares: I'm not moving. Amid all possible co-
ordinates, dying in one place.

☯

Only the words which survive passage through silence, only those.
The words no longer words. Walls arise around me from nowhere,
rise nowhere and are not there. Coordinates are all walls like these:
the strength and nonsense of sheer air. I refuse their being there. The
word made flesh becomes silence, the dark sheath of earth through
which a subterranean river flows. The word made flesh in the cool
stone hallways becomes the blind white fish. In the darkness by
the water in the echolalic rooms, things become no-things: races

no longer tantamount to the infinite fields of tombs. Current, the biceps of water, just under the skin of change: exercise, sheer exercise, between no now nor then, my empty hand in the darkness closes, then opens again.

Where some unenvisaged things have vanished, there is no passage. I am inside this woman inside me, a changing darkness from my own black light. Through my hollowest centre streams the subterranean river, darker, deeper and more silver than clearest remembrance of height in air. Around me the albino fish who lost long ago the need for eyes and eyes. Through the cool stone hallways this float into inlet into inlet into pool receiving pool.... The quiet is coming and the dark. The river, she knows, is flowing close. I know and know eddying close to certain darker of the walls. Somewhere distant a drop is falling from the nippled pool high on the cool ceiling. Rings widening on the surface pass through her and through the stone membranes of these walls and walls of walls. A drop has fallen. The river knows. The river is all rings like this. It flows and does not flow. Far darker now— gone, the waving stone columns, continuous pillars in this temple of the dead — but I sense them passing, eyes-needle, needleeye, through I thread like the river— never touching — as it wall after wall inside her threads. When will I go with the blind white fish in search of an absence of eyes?

The beast who sleeps at the ends of the optic nerves, stirs, wakens, looks for me in the labyrinth of my consciousness. It's he—it—who causes the drop to fall. Who steps impossibly through the membranes of stone. His descendants form no chain. I'm his opposite: emptiness contained.

☯

Only the albino fish survives time, darkness, absence of eyes. I must open my eyes to colour as if light has never been. Fire is the absence here.

❧

An intentional amnesia causes the clarity of this aesthesia. Have I been always at the centre of a subterranean river? I gave to receive, received to give, learned at the last instant of living: It is impossible to live.

❧

An eye alone in passage fangles laws with one end: to break them. Watch and compass lost, my fingers rove the wallways for a stone. I cause the woman who causes me, the word between words - one hieroglyph of nerve and blood. This place is and is not the same. I become the subterranean river that becomes me. I become these walls that become me. I become this woman who answers to my name. The only vision is in clear black light. Colours begin which sleep within the walls. An animal comes to the water's edge and eases in, the water deeper than the wish. Now, if never again, I am the blind white fish.

❧

Rams of the sea butt the sea-cliffs unenthusiastically. West, the last light goes close against the swells. The fat bear and fewer insects of August are sinking, and a single consciousness balances on the deck listing softly left and right. In a few years — I won't be here — an earthquake will rearrange these proportions, but this evening the light is moving among the houses on pilings that clutch to the cliff-wall, two legs in the sea. Nothing stirs. And this boat is an empty container. A shack draws my gaze, for no reason. Simply my sight has come to rest there upon that shamble verandah. The whole thing drops into the water — I'm too far out for noise — and the waves go like sharks for the pieces and bear them toward Japan. Between the breakers, no drowning hands wave. A home is gone. No one has noticed. No commotion on the shore, and I'm not alarmed. The cliff-face shows no sign that ever a shack clung there and I won't tell anyone. Some years ago this was told to me, but today it is as true as the truth of a later earthquake which shoveled into the sea all the boats and houses of that landscape.

All my days to come are hung like drying char upon a pole. To exceed both celebration and remorse is to become machine, the merest mindless organism that comes from the sea to strive toward certain death upstream. For nothing it will survive to remember. Among these arctic isles of mind, the water, in summer, is very much the colour of stone; in the winter, land is the colour of water. It's winter, I find, most of the time. Break-up is less and less significant change. I'm learning how to dread that shift of surfaces, my fine numb continuum deranged. The dead seals of this morning's consciousness roll bloated and tied together, half in the water, half on the sand. What is there but to shoot or harpoon when a seal or a metaphor surfaces? Yet these carcasses are neither what I saw nor what I meant.

These are the poisoning grounds, here where the birds nest at the northern terminus of the long flight. It would be hard to see from the air, if planes flew in this direction. The reek of carrion is overwhelming. Bones and flesh are dissolving into the earth. Only the feathers live on beyond the rest of living the things that made them fly. There are few flies or other insects; presumably they die too like the foxes and shrews whose skeletons have joined those of the ducks and geese. The occasional moose or bear blunders here. After the long, slow death is over and the sea-flats have received these fauna and flora, what are these shadow shapes inside me stepping through putrefied grounds with their bags of quill and down?

I'm nothing who dreams the something with whom the world dreams itself in contract. Moses ascends the volcano through the summer dusk. In his hands: a stone-chisel and a heavy hammer. After the sounds of his footsteps seep into the muskeg, I'm drawn only by the distant invasions of icebergs calving into the invisible sea, and the view of wounds approaching across the ice, black water bleeding forth along my way. All the opposites have gone golden, and I've almost forgotten left and right.

J. Michael Yates

☯

Yes, the wise seething of these flies, as I come upon the mandible of a big, big animal — off-white here in the off-green of thick weeds. Nothing else remains of the structure. The wolves and porcupines have forgotten, my life shifts weight from foot to foot, and the flies and I could soon come to an understanding. I've dined upon death and know the uses of spreading disease. It's my choice: this is the jawbone of an ass. I might pick it up and flush something to slay. No, it's the chin and rotten teeth of Fred Nietzsche who died so far north of himself that no one bothered to look for his remains. Toward the last, he grew great antlers and spent most of his time alone at the edges of the high lakes eating the white young buds of water-lilies. The wolves pulled him down from inside, then ate skinward. I defer to flies; there's nothing left to live on for long, unless it's possible, for a little while, to subsist on merely seething. Say simply something died somewhere in the weeds, and this is left, this engine he used to try to eat what ate him.

☯

I've been right here, in the air, without scaffolding, turning expertly at coruscate nuts, lock-washers, ends of mammoth bolts at all my contiguations. Farther down than I could see, girders and beams struck and reverberated a long time up the faces of the air around me. It was good at last to come around to what at last was good to come around to. Side by side and storey by storey, I unbuilt toward the centre. I'm sitting in sheer air now - very slowly, very reflectively, bending back and forth now and then, just a little, the flared feet of the last cotter-key.

☯

One totem demands: When the father grows feeble and contributes no longer to the stores, the eldest son shall lead him far over the sea ice, and there at the black water's edge, do him to death. And another:

The father shall slay the son who raises his hand against him. *This winter sky is the blue roof of an open mouth that chews ceaselessly.*

Again and again I go away from you and send back only words. Where I am is very cold and the ice figures I collect for you never, somehow, survive the transport. And so these small black tracks upon the page. Where you are is too warm for me. This message is a map which shows my exact coordinates at this moment. Follow it. Try to find me. I should like to be here when you arrive, but in this weather it is necessary to keep moving.

I dream cautiously, as if between high peaks heavy with avalanches. Seventy-seven days a year the ice concedes small craft upon the water here. Call it ratio of animal to angel. Beneath their infinite sky of ice, the fish dream a slow sound of breaking. When passage hardens between banks, and numbers speak for seconds and for years: cautiously, in my underwater light, I dream the fish.

A dredge like this can bite a mountain down. It eats almost everything — all the scrub-pine for miles around in its boilers, water from the stream-bed it follows to make its own steam and the pond on which it floats always forward. Ahead of it the rocks are different shapes and colours. Pieces in the tailing piles behind are very much the same size and, strangely, the colour of rust. Here and there, their long necks rise out of gullies silhouetted against the crimson and indigo winter light like the skeletons of extinct reptiles stopped in the midst of feeding. Only these frozen, level wastes remain and hulls of the machines that made them. The men who made the machines are gone, and the gold, and this anachronistic, inefficient method of mining.

The moon is closer to the earth in the north of the northern hemisphere. I'm here to be closer to the light which happens in the dark. I've ascertained that the moon is the skull of a deceased deity, viewed from above. Deep pits mar the surface: these can be explained: peckmarks from the starved scavenger birds of space which roost in the vacuum between planets. I can say now that the moon is black or green, by turns, occasionally both simultaneously (a nameless colour), and the light of the moon comes from no source other than its core. A single candle burns there now at that centre where the mind of a god once served no purpose whatsoever. It breathes, inspires, the moon does; the halitosis of the moon is overwhelming.

Ideas decoyed and then out-stalked him. He lay at night disbelieving brute possibility: in mind, now, he had committed all the inhuman things. All walls down, everything lay at his mercy: this laid him sacrifice at the feet of even the weakest things.

Daily she came less and less cautiously for the small food I held in the finger-tips of my words. By the time I had completely disarmed her suspicion, her strength had increased through my feeding: I dared not attempt to seize her. Now, mornings she leaves to forage in the streets for me: we wait as I ready myself to attempt anything her blood waits to resist.

That earth turns, I have no objection, but how it turns concerns me. If only the atmosphere didn't turn too, I could have the air of China at one time of day, that of France at ' another, and so with all possible places, with a few latitudinal revisions. However, the air of noon is very much the air of midnight. Sunday bulges with Thursday's air. My lungs fill with the weather of ten years ago. An atmosphere of every breath I've ever taken follows me everywhere over the earth. In this dimension, I've lived every second of my history in precisely one place.

This is my receipt for death: I'm swimming hard in arctic water, moving away from all shores, diving deep to feed and rising less and less often for air. I've copulated in open water and seen all the seal islands and migrated here and there with the herds that move mindlessly and bleed a single blood when slaughter comes in ships full of clubs, when death comes through the maw of a very white bear. I'm swimming hard in arctic water, then a fleet of kayaks behind me. In them: eskimos of a sort that perhaps never were — creatures I shall have to imagine. Then a good chase and a good harpoon, then to drown in fathoms of my own making. And nothing shall be wasted: oil for dryfish, fur for clothing, bones for fishhooks and jewelry. My heart and my eyes go as prize for the first harpoon. And the head: the head to the waiting dogs.

A man, warmly dressed, in perfect health, mushing his dogs a short distance between two villages, never arrives. He has forgotten to reach down, catch a little snow in his mitten and allow it to melt in his mouth. For a reason neither he nor his dogs understand, he steps from the runners of his sled, wanders dreamily — perhaps warmly, pleasantly — through the wide winter, then sits to contemplate his vision, then sleeps. The dogs tow an empty sled on to the place at one of the two villages where they're usually fed. While those who find the frozen man suspect the circumstance of his death, always they marvel that one so close to bed, warmth, food, perhaps family, could stray so easily into danger.

☯

Beaver. I become this: outraged by the perpendicularity of the trees, and set about hewing all things erect horizontal. Then the even more terrible order: the breakneck narrow torrent of mine strangles and widens into the dam of my dreams. The rush of things retards in paternoster pools. And now, in the windless water, the fish see too much. They grow wary, then overwary, and then wary only. Should the shadow of a spruceclaw pass across the bottom or a leaf fall upon the surface, they petrify into objects lost in the subaqueous landscape. Silt deepens until the rocks are no longer visible, and every movement of mine stirs up clouds of filth, and there is nothing further to become for safety. After a time the fish tremble even at the sounds of other fish piercing the surface for flies.

I no longer believe in what I don't know about cities, but there's still something in open country and clear deep water that draws me. Because I fear to know: knowledge of something attractive only in its enigma is terrible. That sweet small darkness is going away as I return and return and cannot but return. I turn to this tangled landscape as a man turns to a woman and dream that because I haven't been here before, neither has any other man.

Today I've been a race of men - engineers, all of us, aloft on the giddy scaffolding which covers the stone faces of the Tower of Babel like a net of enormous mesh. Soon we'll sleep. And die in our sleep. I'll awaken as the Abraham of a new people. A busy people. We'll be busy burying those who died during the night. Some of us will excavate the mammoth common graves. Others will tend the cremation ovens. Still others will explain carefully and patiently to those who refuse both burial and burning. This last employment, conversations with corpses that will not lie down, is, finally, the central activity. Never do they understand, nor we, why they don't understand.

The salmon circle a spawn, crimson in clear emerald. There's a time not to eat anymore. To go against the current until the end swims beside you tirelessly. There's a time for the great bear who waits at the turn of the water to take the body and all its possible generations in a single sweep. But to go aground on the shallows, side up, not living and not dead, to oil the air with rot ... with every orbit around perpetuity, a little more flesh falls away.

I watched the bear too long — until my face became that of a bear watching a man. It happened with the salmon as well: my lower jaw grew into a great hook, a hump rose on my back, I reddened until I look like fire under the water on my way upstream. I'm waiting at the stream-side, claw under the current. Around rocks, through the shallows, back out of the water, decaying, I'll be there, because there is nothing to do but arrive.

At freeze-up and break-up the suicides occur. It's part of the weather —as much outside us as the seasons. Summer and winter are commitments, velocities. During the long light or the long dark, we watch one another arranging our odds. who'll eat the end of his shotgun this fall? And how about me? At freeze-up the pliant things we depend on go solid. At break-up the icebridges we've gotten used to give way. There's no word from outside because the ice is too thick for planes with pontoons and too thin for planes with skis. Boats are beached. Either the snow is too thin for dogs and snowmobiles or going soft, rotten and spotty. You can't work for the mud and uncertain ground at both times of the year. You can only go inside and wait it out. You never know when there'll be nothing there.

J. Michael Yates

FROM PARALLAX

Death like a parachute collapsing.

The clown with two revolvers, one to his temple, the other between your eyes.

And no one to note the quality of simultaneity, and I mean only electrically when I speak of the electrical fields.

❡

Death, too, is arrangement,

This war of words between the lens which composes and the lens which records.

I take this life to illustrate what

I won't be in the picture to verify.

❡

There is at least one indestructible negative.

❡

The photograph come uncemented from its dimensions is a man - except that it survives.

Beyond my last sense of wilderness first wilderness begins.

The poisons I take to poison my poisons.

To whom say the end?

I want the blossom of doom and none of its seeds.

How to begin a theory of warning.

Fireweed after the burn. It is the fireweed I'm waiting for.

☯

In this city of suicides and no storms, it is never hot nor cold. I can depend on the landscape. Except for the fogs. And then I'm busy with the foghorns. Beginning. to see.

When one shape falls away from the mobile, there begins a sharp list at the left hand of the sea.

Being takes doing between its teeth and begins, like a crazed retriever, to shake.

I leave off, always, precisely as the moment becomes a partially-painted room.

☯

A small room gone strange with distances: my hand engaged at a green machine on another coast in another country. A continent of time between.

Words are better than talk and silence better than words.

The pane of this window is everywhere.

Nowhere at all, its frame.

☯

Beneath a bridge of silence passes the night ferry:

A hive of lights translating toward the high convex of a strong lens.

Design spans the vacuous light between one blackness and the next.

Seeing is clear isobar - the line I don't draw through all points which have the same consciousness for a given period of space.

Some sounds are beyond the range of the eye's ear.

I grow fingers between my fingers.

Light-leaks in the darkroom, the fungus of explanation.

❧

I begin to notice the landscape which has always been there. Always, because it has always been possible. Never inevitable.

How to live more than one life at once.

How to see, to become, at once, more than one thing.

Precision: the labyrinth of what I say and the Minotaur of what, unsaid, sleeps at the ends of my optic nerves.

❧

Beyond black, worms of love-talk snarl in a ball at the centre of the carpet. Hollowness inside the bronzes hardens and the sights of breaking fill the last spaces between birds.

A slow halide fire in my head becomes eyes of then in the face of now.

How to die without wasting anyone's time. How to process what has never happened before.

This is a way to renounce time and space. Not to forget them.

I own what I change. Or it clings to me.

The fingers grow long memories into the stale air of a room.

The infinity sign is ours: a hieroglyph whose two worlds die into one another at a station perceptible to neither, nor any outsider.

Each wing of the luminous insect takes its life from the other.

One says: two circles which fangle a third figure.

One suspects: this is one circle twisted once upon itself.

HONGYUN

The figure knows: permanence in motion, situations of light moving over the systems of black water, the black contingencies of this small air.

How to discover red in a small dark room.

How to avoid injuring the dark.

☯

What grows out of blackness is still blackness. Light: blackness out of key with the eye.

Zero's memory of the future begins to short-circuit — a firefly at the sill of a long, hot, humid night.

Occasionally, from a dark corner of the darkroom, there arrives a print of the sound of time-bergs calving into a cold sea.

These are the moraines.

☯

The last woman was a green light passing over my skin, a rising water, a wheel of coloured beams through a fountain changing shape. Fountains irrigate nothing. Nothing grew. Like a poisonous plant.

Not reality, but arrangement: this horde of changes I name I and I and I.

In the tank in the water in the dark, the dissonant merge of content and intent, the grand animal of accident.

☯

At once both sides of the lens constitutes one reproduction or another. Something with a will toward duration that is not me.

Tomorrow only the darkness was alive.

Death in dim amber light lingers at the brink of a flat pan and there rinses a lemur in amber chemical. The animal will not revive.

The substance of vacuum is infinite. Labyrinth dangles from the sky like a mobile through which there moves a camera. Or its precise counter-weight.

Every radar is solitary: the presence made of absences which navigates the instantaneous isles of light.

Not the object but the feel of the impulse upon it; take back what goes out, it's a life; try never to sell more life than I can afford to buy back.

The light changes.

The eye changes.

Between, a changing screen, the slight film between living and the null.

Over the high peaks at the middle range, the chartreuse flower of flame is coming. Thereafter, only the shriek of a single bird: the sound of a gigantic machinery, out of control, precisely.

Voice follows through a dim tree of rooms like slow certain fire through a dry skull.

The metamorphic zones: a green dryness is growing up the grass.

The final camera's camera is the camera, the seeing thing I don't see because it is whatever sees.

This self-conscious nothing is another hole in the air and in the light.

Wind bends better than the light.

The courage to expose without film is what I'm waiting for.

Everything the other side of the madman's lens is now.

The shutter opens to record the open shutter.

Mirrors speak more and more with the eyes of an absence that has seen some splendid animals.

Destructive, these creative loves exceed the sad seep of a century over the lip droops into the laugh of an idiot.

Whether the dancer ages in mid-leap, history is busy somewhere the other side of the window.

Death's life locates in the magma of its idea.

Numberless, the ways of starvation.

I speak to the elephant smell at the middle of my back where I can't sleep. The left hand only dreams the right. The mirror dreams both hands. History dreams a man, a prototype that never reaches production. I dream that I dream that I dream.

Only the infinite camera focuses at infinity.

Meanwhile you are dying and I am dying and we aren't together.

A vehicle at deep speed is another silence full of lives.

It is the film which slips the sprocket at mid-moment, I'm waiting for.

Every form must become a precise self-destroying machinery, a green fireworks over black water, a movement at the sill of peripheral vision, an irreversible reaction.

A firestorm bulges over the perimeters of the focal plane.

J. Michael Yates

A green fish streaks through the no-name solution into which consciousness, like crystals, disappears.

☯

I know by the sound of my breathing that it is no longer within my control. A giraffe is burning in the far right range of the indigo plane.

The telescopic man in the wide-angle silence examines his hands. Astern: the loud absence of all the rudders of history.

Cataracts begin again over the eyes in my finger-prints.

☯

A nascent tiresome madness is moving through the crowd at the verge.

My life ... my death, toward which timber does the fire pendulate?

One reel of the long film runs reverse always.

☯

While eyes — gone green over the green glow of the radar screen - follow the sweep of light, the craft goes aground ... sunk by a two-dimensional danger no eye has ever seen.

The machinery did not see itself, its presence too central, too invisible on the screen.

Focus takes a life of its own— desire of the eye to become a lens, desire of the lens to become an eye— a fine death badly mauled by rage, a hand alone with a full pen and an empty page.

Tomorrow morning in the darkroom: rise of another night. Behind it the rising of a night in the mirror that rises before the shutter sees.

At the point of partial commitment to suicide that results in whole death, I leave off. And at the verge of total desire that ends in the half-act.

HONGYUN

FROM INSEL: THE QUEEN CHARLOTTE ISLANDS MEDITATIONS

This winter in which you find me is not your winter.

☯

Because things much more dangerous than death remain unreined by names, they cannot, like island horses, be broken.

Nor shot to part them from their pain.

☯

When the colourless hand of fog closes over the coast, it is not death, but it is not living.

☯

Preferring to bide its opposite, things bide time instead.

☯

Time to fangle, time to become a beach between at least two more and more unequal distances.

☯

There are choices: Become a larger fisherman. Or a fisherman smaller. The boats lengthen or grow shorter. And fewer. Always fewer.

☯

Begin fishing in deep winter. Go landless, navigate your vessel away from all harbours, have a go at the high ocean rollers.

☯

J. Michael Yates

After an unknown number breaks over the bow, expect the ice to begin and win and win until everything above water-line overbalances like a hydrocephalic child.

☯

At the capsize comes an easing of decision: when the hands blue and loosen, when the jagged air is to no further point, when none cries out to no one in fear any longer, and none pauses to warn, and the northern night settles down in its blackness to a coast of a few smug lighthouses and a few dimly interrogative horns.

☯

I can see more than one snowpeak from this beach. Alaska. On a lucid day.

Something of me, on the move always, busy in more than one time, in more than one place.

Sound of a seaplane approaching from somewhere above the cover.

Footsteps of a stone-age tribe of shellfish-eaters coming toward me in bad darkness and in bad light going away.

And no word will speak exactly one stone subtracted from all possible beach.

☯

You are forward. I am aft. Control of the outboard engine is mine. You've brought your thirty-ought-six fishing to blow hell out of dogsharks that might nuisance our lines. In the service of commercial fishermen, you will kill; in memory, possibly, of drowning sailors clinging to rocks; for the future of small children wading the shallows of the saltchuck almost anywhere.

Tide failing, and over your right shoulder, on my left, I notice the rock full of sea-lions and seals that foul and rob the nets of commercial fishermen, screw up the gill-netting in the middle of a perfect run, and commit other high marine crimes, and I nose us

158

HONGYUN

toward them keeping your face toward me. knowing that any second the herd will decide that we are we and judder back down the rockside into the water and dive, goddammit, dive, and don't come up for air until you're miles from here.

Their fact comes and goes away without your knowledge and saltspray chewing all the pretty off your gun. You sip your beer and squint at the rod-tips as we troll.

I don't love God's creatures nor even God. No. And, yes, I had to come all this distance and partly become you over all these years to learn I loathe a part of your imbecile, Canadian northbilly soul.

☯

At the sandy graveside, looming thunderheads of words close away the light.

Thus the sea breathes in, easily, one more long and negligible history.

Before the land writes one man, it blots a thousand thousand.

☯

Child, may you never notice that seabirds, electrons, and galaxies are also only words.

☯

Pulse unsteady at the speed of dark.

Do not attempt to catch falling objects. Especially debris of failing light.

When the full ovoid moon of my demon squints over the horizon of reason,

When I have come north as far as I can come,

There remains only, without watch, without compass, entrance into the calling wild.

J. Michael Yates

Loosing of the mind to hunt the mind amid the shadowy talus of lightscape.

❧

Don't let them do it under cover of darkness.

They will do it in any case, but don't let them, dammit, do it in the dark.

To defy gods, to glory them, and in spite of us, they will do it.

But let us pact and cause them to do what they do in our light,

That one or two might notice and recall the price of nothing at all.

❧

This winter in which you find me is not my winter.

It doesn't fit. And neither can be altered.

Take it away.

❧

What lingers here still hushes and gives on the wind:

Intimation of another time when these same cedars whittled grand men into frightened little boys.

How to have known these silences independent of my noise.

❧

At sudden places, through this tree-tunnelled way toward Rose Spit and the ease of land, a plank road — hand-fitted, ancient — insists through the sand like a battle won in a war long, long ago, lost.

❧

Now and then the citizen wins a battle. Reluctantly. Humbly. But the madman of me loves the whole war.

☯

No, not innocence, I have not come north again to recover an innocence of which I slaved to be rid. It is my sacred worthlessness I wish to exhume.

☯

Island north is new and not new to me. What is new, perhaps, lives only in the view, vision, sight, standing calf-high in cougar-coloured grass from a sea-cliff hill between Skidegate and Tlell, through wind sharp as a d-adze, toward Cormorant Rock. The dark basalt alive with things which cock and fire their necks of S-shape spring and open and close their in and out of water wings.

Their purpose — these blots of rock, these bent animals, this carver's wind — is not clear. Sometimes it has to be enough. To be. Merely. To be. Here. Squirt by squirt of the heart.

Time and tide, exhaling here, now, after the long breathing-in of being young. Here on the subsiding side of both time and tide, among the clear pools full of things waiting for water to return, the steel-coloured sea-blade carving far out and almost out of sight, falling and falling and almost at low-slack. Time now to say inside it is almost good to know for a certainty with the blood: I can die. With luck, the tide of knowing won't rise to the brain for a little while longer. And inhale. And remember: there was a woman I once cared for most when she most smelled of northern low tide.

What enters the amber eye of the cormorant never reaches an organ which thinks or tries to think or cares that a dark figure across the blowing water atop a seahill stands there trying to think about not thinking, carefully not voicing a postulate such as: I don't think, therefore I am not. This is a possibility which, possibly, even I could care about.

J. Michael Yates

☯

Those who come to these islands come in fright, come from frightening places to here which, frightening as it is, seems less frightening, for a little while, than every other frightening place.

☯

Like geese and teal and widgeon and certain other animals of water and air, certain of us pause from flight here, uncertainly, to eat and drink whatever there is, to fuck what is now and then willing, or doesn't, momentarily, care — then, again, fly.

☯

Evidence of my having been somewhere sometimes takes on the appearance of life. In times of luck, news arrives several stops behind me.

☯

Flight was never a way of life. Neither was life in the nesting.

☯

I don't remember the rest, but her letter thus came to the end of itself: my body, however pretty, is disposable; not so, the rest, I don't care who I fuck so long as who I fuck doesn't.

☯

Flight is the solitary goose-cry in the night of being frightened of all but one thing.

☯

Getting elsewhere is one way of not staying and, with luck, not saying: I can't stay here anymore and there's no understanding to it; with luck, not lying: I'll see you, this place, again, later, again, it's been good, I'm only leaving for a sojourn, I won't be long, I'll call, I'll write, the time will pass, yes, yes, very quickly; not, with luck, saying to myself: thus it begins again, the flow which folds me in and drowns on toward the lightless sea-floor at the end of all further places to go.

🌑

Out of flight, I try and again try to coax a way of life.

Goddamn the part of the heart opposed to this.

Of escape I make a place to live. Almost. Not quite. I am full of this certainty: surely not all of escape has been staked, subdivided, occupied.

🌑

Accidentally, I am blowing out the lantern of what I know with the black breath of what I cannot possibly.

🌑

Love of edge. Have lived it. Always I have lived toward love of edge, of the gleaming, of the treasured blade of nothing , its voyage through sapwood toward the core, the fleet wedge of used beauty to be driven between the dead ends of duty, ending, after the back-cut, in spent gaze which fixes on the fall: doors of gravity opening, gravity rising to claim. Gravity, receiving.

🌑

…I'm serious about the whales, Jack Gilbert

🌑

Fluke. Seamark for a vanishing point: thus, then, these flukes fan, undreamable sheening this evening without evening breeze.

Somewhat sunset, somewhat silhouette, rooted somewhere unreasonable beneath the salt skin of sea; bole, twin mammoth fronds; one sense invents the scent of prehistoric flora.

J. Michael Yates

This evening empty of evening breeze, the living kingdoms merge: half an animal mirages half a tree.

☯

Lake surrounded by land surrounded by sea.

Archaic water. Colour of peat whisky. So used, the fabric of surface begins wearing through.

So many things, some much like lives, enter their beauty only while dying. Or ill. Or supposing.

☯

The mind swings like the needle of a compass between sentences of treatment and sentences of punishment.

The hand upon the power-saw is undeterred. The alder and fireweed springing back to reclaim what belongs to a wilderness are undeterred.

Everything is winning.

And none.

North is the heaviest judgement of a wilderness upon a mind. Prison is the heaviest judgement on the mind by what a wilderness is not.

Unless the mind consents, whereupon the sense of sentence rearranges itself, and what or who judges vanishes into ice-fog or into whiteout or into mist.

At a certain extreme of extremity, all sentences, formal and informal, interchange.

The case does not rest.

☯

In this geography of north the language of north is understood by almost all. And spoken by almost none.

164

HONGYUN

☯

Here, it is possible to grow so preoccupied with the detail of the environment that one forgets it is to live in.

☯

Far, deep, away in the south of my time alive, I condense the many into one redwing blackbird whose stray voice

Deeper and deeper seeps through the high, fuzzing cattails of my fisher youth:

Old now, silent now, the creature is captive still inside the collapsing boyhood of dream.

Collapsing.

That fine capture of golden animal light.

☯

I have failed to cure my compass of north and the needle no longer homes there in any way known to me.

Like houses of cards, tall towers of importances collapse and reorganize themselves here.

How one arrives here has little to do with how mainland minds move from one place to another place.

What can be taken for granted — these tones of uncertainty — are not what one takes for granted in the place called *outside*.

The ways to die are extraordinary by terms of ordinary lives

So it is with insular north and with prison. In these places, even the unusual must be approached unusually. For survival, the routine must come to seem extraordinary. Commonplace: the extreme.

I have come to know -the complicated way - sanctuary in surroundings of terror. That a world through the wrong end of the telescope is also a world. That I prefer not to die among the hordes dying of safety.

Certain things can persist only in the languages of what they are not.

Certain things are as they are, like powerlines: held definite only by their bonds, with or without consent.

A north.

A prison.

Mere ideas, therefore not dangerous until expressed. And for a few, not dangerous even then.

Mere forms which feed on the energy of fantasy; therefore delicate and they starve to death easily.

Two of numberless steamy windows opening on a nameless metaphor.

He was one who had come to love dark. He surmised so. And that he truly allowed his process through the long, soft gut of darkness, the singular peristalsis of aurora, all senses circulating close, like the blood of cold.

His life had become a refinement of the art of remaining merely metabolic, and when death came to him again and again, he didn't give a damn whether to woof or bite.

When lowest temperature arrived and kicked the struts out from under what it is that holds refuse aloft in the sky of the skull, he could see clean - almost - through to the timeward border of infinity.

North, deep north. Poseidon, landlord of water, skulks the sands of island coast - sulking. Seeming fearful. Strangely despairing of his seas.

HONGYUN

An oilslick translates itself from the surf to the sand beneath his feet. This spotted serpent of beach coils ninety miles without intrusion of right-of-way.

The data of north is no longer flowered.

Unlike its bewildered history.

☯

Only in angry rapture, might a god carve this voluptuous killer terrain.

☯

The ones here whose nicknames I learn, the ones who die almost daily of wilderchine, of the place where bush and mechanical behemoth no longer exist independent of one another: these who die here take less and less of me away with them to their uncharted archipelago of darkness, but leave this increasing reef which is visible only at minus tide of the memory.

☯

It is not that island time means more dimly than all other time.

It is that the form and energy of this island Yakoun River resemble the breath and depth of no other river.

Because of Yakoun time, nothing is landlocked. There are no non-sea-run fish. No non-sea-run dreams. All things living, eventually, voyage toward the sea. Nothing is landlocked here. Except, possibly, a man consenting. Possibly a man like me.

Time here frequently suspends. Or slows toward cease, as all sound seems to cease when, dim and deep in the interior spell, the drumming of a single grouse erases the huge boom of a falling seven-hundred-year-old spruce.

☯

Deeper than sapwood, I could become something almost authentic among these numberless colours of green. Except for the No in me that remains inaccessible, high on a steep sidehill somewhere.

Better this decided distance; better to smoke a cigarette in order to keep something between island and me; better to say one word aloud, alone; better to leave one boot-print in the wet memory of volcano.

No.

I could undress, conceal myself, and, like all else here, transpire. Breathe. Simply breathe.

Today, one or more will say: The view is beautiful, simply beautiful.

And that's right. And that's all. Today is merely beautiful. A drunk for the senses and offense to imagination.

Distance is not without mercy.

No.

Some will suppose it fear. Still: No.

Never, perfectly, will this moment in this place exit me.

And there is no way for me quite in.

❧

As the wharves zipper together land and water, hold on. Hold it together. For the quick, forever is not long. *Dad?* Yes. *Can you come to this island where I am?* I hope so. *Soon?* I'll try. *The day after today?* Soon. *It's very dark where I am, you know?* I think I can remember. Can you come here and held with the dark? I think.... *Can you?... come?... help?* I will. *What can you do?* I'll think of something. *When?* Before the pontoons touch the beach right in front of where you are. *Dad?* Yes. *Well, it's dark right now where I am, you know?* I'll think of something. *But couldn't you think right now? Instead?*

❧

HONGYUN

Inside the dark body of the real, what I point to only resembles what I think it is, what you accept it as, what we hang a word on, then a diminutive; then the invocation with forced fearlessness, lion-tamer's familiarity.

There are the words.

There are the things.

There I am working both sides of the street, trying to bang a life out of confusing the two.

The words were never the things. Things had to be before words. My body was before its noun. Nouns tend to lie down together: with luck, my noun with your noun through the good service of a hardy verb.

There is an office of time which links unnamable, named things.

Reason is certain that things must have been before syllables to signify in their stead. The Dawson Caribou before its moniker, then the volumes of extinct to fill the places of its insular absence.

Something not reason is not at all certain. Something somewhat God.

Words in their own lives insist on being things. And things are never quite things until they wear names. This leads the mind again circular into the dark body of suspicion. A word might, at least once, antecede a thing, might turn flesh, turn light, and enter a comprehensive body of the dark.

☯

Announce the environment has been settled: the dam will go up on schedule. With a hole in the centre to allow the river to run through.

☯

What confirms life can kill. And will.

☯

169

He loved wine.

No wine entered him.

It was necessary to remain steadily ready for the gods of darkness to exceed their drunken shiftlessness and arrive.

He died not drunk but hungry. Without knowing whether he had ever been ready. Without knowing whether his summons had ever been served.

Much scotch has gone into me. Now none.

The gods show and no-show as it pleases them.

I awaken to the sound of a pen gouging a page. No memory of entrance into the drunk.

Hours and months pass for which - other than this - I have no account at all.

❦

I have been a war.

When I'm over, who will there be to despair over the evidence, to bury the fallen moss-chandeliers which come to resemble parts of things human which come to resemble, sometimes, something more.

Who to burn the treaties.

Who to reconstruct the space and cleanse it.

And who, cool and healing, to overweave my fireperforations of the silence?

Footing once firm on the wharf gives the quick twitch and sag of danger.

Something has to be done about something from time to time to time.

My good madness strays. My good madness malingers among things cast up by suck of moon and things cast down by me not soon enough.

In the sea-noon light, a strut falls away, beneath a wharf built to weather and stay put beyond all face-lifts of land and all quick decisions of evil-mooded sea.

An old dog, crazed by being both dog and old, looses its life upon the sand, scattering the scatter of time and water, until it finds and rolls tirelessly in the high carcass of bits unfit for touch by even the farthest finger-tips of mind.

Nothing is behind it all.

I spy it sometimes peering around the corner of my eye as I bend down to reach for an urgent shape of drift or draw back to send a stone back into the breakers, giving it — for an instant — a life unlike all other stones.

Perhaps, around the next headland, or the next, I'll turn and —for an instant — face nothing, no longer hedging just beyond the rim of a motorcycle mirror nor dodging among sun-glitzed motes of dust in a room at the line between dusk and deep afternoon, but face nothing square-on for the first time. Or first, seemingly.

Around the next headland: perhaps just beyond a hollow drift-log I'll rig a photograph of myself inside (to prove to me I was both there and then), perhaps near the skeleton of mahogany decking of a ship killed there more than fifty years ago, still sinking through beach, bow accusing the sky still, like Laocoon.

J. Michael Yates

Then, around the next headland, I'll go on. And forget for all purposes of words exactly what I've seen. And know, as uselessly as before, exactly what I've known.

☯

Dear Outside:

No, please do not come here. Something has happened. Things as they were between me and what is not me are not as they are.

The craft threads through islands without tree, free of human evidence, but swarmed by white birds.

There are birds of other colours. One sees the white.

The birds see three-hundred- sixty degrees, and possibly degrees without assigned numbers.

There is a refuge in nakedness and exposure to terrible weather.

☯

Inside the river, rocks roll over and disclose their dark, wet unders.

Beneath them, everything dies of travel and light.

Look up. Check the geese. Go the other way.

☯

When I touch selected surfaces: carved soapstone, certain places of uncertain women, dark argillite curve, the grip of a tool by flesh worn smooth: my fingertips do what my eyes do when they stare.

☯

In the mind-light of braiding river time, I was a minor incident between no longer and not yet.

☯

Follow this way through the dark curtain of rain. It will take you
to his cabin. It is the only one there, you can't miss it, there on the
edge where yes and no contiguate. There may or may not be a light
on. If not, think in tungsten: the filament burnt far too soon for the
price, but the vacuum still perfectly performing. Inside it is dry. Stay
the night or part of it. The roof sags with weight of moss and wet.
The structure is old as it looks. Here, weather accounts for virtually
everything.

Here, beyond the small sand mountain at the edge of the reserve,
time tilts diagonal. Ordinary turns unusual. Certainty comes over
me that this windy light is nowhere but here... and like ... nothing...
other than whatever it appears... to me... right now ... right here.
As if from somewhere above, excarnate, I see me seated on the third
silvered step before the carver's home watching consciousness embody
as breeze in the dune-grass flow.

That dried black crop hanging up there above the stove? Seaweed.
Indian food. Make you fart like on old dog... it's good for you. You
white guys don't fart enough. There's an old saying up here: Never
follow a Haida into a pub toilet in seaweed season.

Mind this: stick to the driftwood when you screw around up near
the spit, eh? Stay off the beach and out of those marsh meadows
where they graze. They can't handle the footing on the driftwood;
that rubbish will save your skin. The farmers brought them. Then
went tits up and left everything. Turned them loose to survive if they
could. That herd of wild cattle has been growing since turn of the
century. More than one dummy has bought it who mistook them for
tame. Smoking, safe here atop the sea's graveyard for logs and trees,
it comes to me what occurs when a life domesticized first faces what
seems simultaneously like itself and strange. Smoke rises as the mist

J. Michael Yates

descends. I'm searching both sides of the interior drift: for anything which, in any case whatsoever, might revert. To anything. At all.

☯

It's an old picture, be careful, no, go ahead, count 'em, twenty-seven men standing on that stump. Not many of those left now. Trees like that. Loggers like that. Only a few of us know where they are, the trees. Never worry about the big weeds on the claim, but stay away from the pole show. The little ones, they look harmless, undercut and drop 'em with a few revs of the saw. But they walk on you, barber-chair on you, they come down quick: the whole tree, drive you into the mud like a nail. Rotten stuff from up top of the big spruce and cedar comes down slow and noisy. You got time to look up and shag ass.

In the toothpicks, you're under before you hear your breath go out.

☯

Whispers live still between the logs which shape the vacancies of this unremembered shelter.

As rot returns this all to wilderness, the voices of rain become less legible.

A thought like a small rodent spirits through a fault of dim memory and goes to repose in the shadow of a sardine-can ashtray in one corner.

The room remembered much until its spine overhead gave in against the wind that batters down a will.

☯

Sea otter carry the uncertain remainder of the species within. Their days rise and die like minus tides beneath moonfire. Before the forces of greed and water, they change. Like seajungle, like the underwater streaming of fur.

☯

Gentian light domes the opaline inlet. Each instant: a diatom of difference. And the eyes of the word never quite enough exact to fix the change.

This vista, too, I shall complicate.

☯

A metabolism gone as still as stone, seemingly not breathing, silent heart ringing anvil blows through tiny bones: this fawn sequestered here in shallow grass, the doe seeing from somewhere I do not see as the fingers of my right hand escape contact with judgement and make contact with the russet fur of a life only just begun.

As the hand returns to me, thought flashes that the doe will never return.

The transparent skin of my scent — odourless to me subtracts this animal from both origin and future.

In the course of almost forty years' passage from one precinct of desert to another, where else has the stink of my finger-prints made septic the unspoiled?

I, who accept that beauty is nothing if not untouchable.

I, whose touch, nevertheless, has browned the petals of many gardenias.

☯

This rising river of answers because I have no Haida questions.

☯

From buried adzes, from a broken yew bow, from strata of shell, they set forth to resuscitate the past... or join it... exactly as it never was, exactly as it never would have been.

☯

Something not yet reported lost is dying with difficulty. Starving.

J. Michael Yates

☯

Hoar-frost whiskers the weather- silvered planking of the wharf. The wharf begins to trouble me, hinged as it is to the edge of the end of land, centipede feet poised on the surface of water, a thing incomplete in wait for the return of something incomplete.

Consciousness nervously blows the pages of memory: The Wanderer... *laena*... lone with o rich and long-drawn-out... *laena*...

The urge to speak of this to someone.

If there was ever anyone, he is missing. And hungry.

At the end of the wharf, even more unease: the aspect of my footprints, dark in light frost, both following, both leading one another in one direction only. *I was a man who trespassed this land when a mirage of unknown still dwelt in the small of his hand.*

☯

One could come, here, to the death of wrath.

To wrath seeping out an uncaulked aperture and all bilge vacuums broken.

The calendar goes end-up and subsides.

No ship on any horizon.

The moongoggled surface of the locofoco sea.

☯

This carving was one of numberless lights in the blood.

The work complies with vision only as body complies with soul.

Body: the sad sack of skin stuffed with death and carnival prizes.

☯

The icecap of knowing somewhat remits.

Dawn features of isle topography like dice cast over the green craps-table surface of the sea by an idle deity.

If not islands, then my register of islands.

On this imperfect skeleton, cure a skin of a few even less perfect lines.

Shipwreck of one of the huge ideas upon an impassable but irresistible reef of language.

Rainbows of fish take up residence and thrive in the derelict hull.

In time, any massive failure can ease under the surface of memory, the glare light of guilt scarring the dark all the way down.

The difference between new and used is useless inside the sea.

Once, the new hulk was an astounding strangeness sinking through the bottomless familiar.

The droplet trapped in the spider skein rocks in thin breeze like a bell which, with every knell, loses presence in the tactile photograph.

Come, Evening: bronze light at the westmost coast of all there is to know.

Light gears down.

The photographer seen between filaments of spider-goods bursts into a frenzy of wrong lenses — without sense that there are focal lengths of fate no lens will accommodate.

Among these silks of shadow, the hands, my hands of water, cannot hold fast any longer.

J. Michael Yates

Capacity to dream an absolute shape of island without means to awaken within it.

ॐ

Infrequently, rage for an open place, for the camouflage of visibility.

Gearing of my insular season engages teeth of the pinion. Sap is stirring in the deadliest trees.

ॐ

To escape the island sickness, travel to the horizon, turn left.

ॐ

Melting light.

A tawn floating toward the ridge-top, very long shot, *Woman, nobody shoots off-hand at three bloody hundred yards. Not even a man,* crosshairs seem to twitch within their circle of collapsing evening.

Settle down and listen: this is about eating.... Killing is the eldest (and probably most constant) human skill.... You put out that old buck's lights, Lady, you offed him and he never knew a thing. If you kill, kill with style as you did just now.

The lousy part of hunting is that the shooter can somewhat initiate but never fully be the time-free beauty of the kill.

The sudden, umbral bloom of sound widens away in a bird-flight of echo.

The strata of silence will recover.

Changed.

ॐ

Agate from pores of a basalt seafloor fall to the beach over the shoulder of a shovelling tide.

HONGYUN

When the day tilts westward, just after a fine rain, after tongues of the Hecate dragon have wearied of flicking the coast with froth and flotsam, at a precise slant of sunbreak an octopus motionless, and scarcely changing colour in its boulder-pool —, then: sight pans to the lacework of crystalline lights strewn across the water-tattooed sand.

Unlinked from mind, the hand begins collecting. Objects heavy and unaesthetic as random can make them. Useless and beautiful, merely, when wet.

☯

Vertical wind, horizontal rain, the affair of warm Japanese current with the air of Alaskan ice.

Here the atmospheric face of a continent is shaped.

Configurations of cloud change from thought to thunder.

At the centre, space more slowly swirls inside outer time.

Senses archive what the will does not.

Plethora and high summer chill.

☯

The high-rigger tops a home-tree.

Then falls with the crown of this plant with which six centuries have not dared meddle.

On his way down, he finds, for the first time, he can plot with absolute accuracy the progress of each travelling part of his body.

☯

Caution near the ones like winter eagles who pause atop only the most high places and glare through the dustless distances.

☯

J. Michael Yates

Stonestroke.

Finally, cutting has whittled to a reason: simply to fondle this love for sharpening.

I glance up through the labour's glow — heavens bloody as the business down below. Across the battlefields of logging slash: only cedar snags. So many, too many, deathtimes still standing.

With each ingenious stroke of steel on stone, ascending toward Hell's grace.

❧

The stain of borrowed time does not wash nor wear free from the fragile fabric of the underbrain.

Sometimes, one dreams, it charms against the sickness of not living.

❧

Lost is another word for ordinary in ordinary insular speech. Islands within the islands will never be mapped. Notion of proportion is small salvation when lost in the head-high salal. While the continuous coast erases and rewrites itself, remember: any river is a system which subdivides not-river into all not-river outside the river and all the rest of the nonriver which is inside the river itself. System explains no other system. Never is a river more than river. Lost is yet another system which declines to self-explain.

❧

More than geography removed: of her, I remember only eyelight. The inerrant dim of an execution chamber. And, like white land birds blooming from an open hamper, will, releasing and releasing. I arrive at the stations of the hours as usual with too much baggage. And immensely over-prepared.

❧

This dream of a captive will letting go: an old and huge sailing craft, loosed from mooring, stiffly shouldering the rollers, under full sail, in full blundering lurch toward open sea.

Then: a lone spinnaker bloom which flaws the otherwise perfect curve of horizon.

☯

Easy, the thought gone dancing to celebrate, the thought gone dancing only to dance, that thought turned dimly, dimly more drunken, a thought entering the wide night for just a little unsmoked air, fresher, very much fresher now, strolling more and more steadily down the frost-whiskered wharf, constellations in this bush place inhaling the eyes, the good sound of solo footsteps on heavy wood ringing out to break against the banks of water-noise to either side. Then the better drunkenness in the best dark at the wharf's end where the sea is seen only by ear, then the phosphor imp, the urge to dive and swim to shore, then reappear a quenched clown at the music... *can't be even a hundred yards between the end of the road and the end of the wharf there. Less from the beach to the end of the wharf depending on your tide. You got maybe twenty seconds this time of year. No one's made it back to beach that anyone remembers. Happens all the goddam time.*

☯

Gauze sky of a maker contemplates its fake in the one-way mirror of sea.

☯

There comes to me nothing to say on behalf of space squandered in search for a primal wilderness.

Fingerprints now cover everything dreamworthy and soon the whole of the galaxy will be second-hand.

J. Michael Yates

These subdued fields cleared by others, I till them always with the thinning hope I'll one day awaken and find them grown up around me - for the first time wild.

❂

I've come here to salvage, to terrorize a consciousness, sunken hugely encrusted in urban coma.

I surround it with peaceless water, then whisper: You cannot swim, don't even dream of it., Summon the last of your small cunning. Become invisible. Become island unnoticed among islands. Think east to the far edge of survival. Think west to a lout defacing blank leisure with form.

A peregrine drops from indigo eternity toward a small animal fleeing in every direction — never before thus bonefrightened, never before thus expansively alive.

❂

For him, parts of island remain tidily *as though* until he breaks parts of his body against them.

Until he breaks his mind against them, the absences exist and exist.

❂

Tlell:

Light goes irresolute and slow, when it shows, and time concealed deep in the light.

❂

Night set. Remembrance of the future in wrath: this chisel is chief among tools of every significant liar. Light pumices all surfaces at the high slack tide of sight. That the spangled fish are in to spawn is never altogether definite. The nets remain, in any case, at ready. What has finally been abandoned becomes an antique photograph, its worth never expressed in a speech of quality, but in one of oblique history.

182

HONGYUN

Surface floats fire— the nervous murk with phosphorous in an easy crescent of tireless waiting. Deeper sparks along the line signal it is all very nearly over.

☯

To this the spooked hope has come: the spell of glacial refugium: a single spit of thought untouched by the last and everlasting cape of ice.

On the evidence of flora nonexistent elsewhere on the skin of the orb. Mushrooms, especially, their changes in the short north summer dark.

On the evidence of certain greens of uncertain moss.

On the evidence of swamp in flames of fern almost impossible to cross.

On the evidence of desire for beyond what hangs from the cedar as certainty.

Transit. Sick. Inglorious.

Noli me tangere… just in case.

Remain far back. Try to go away.

☯

Almost love of a kind for the animals and trees warily enters my hands.

And feeling, definite feeling, for trumpeting, behemoth machines dreamt and driven by old children.

For those who stand tall and speak loudly for geese or for the teeth of gears: nothing in me stirs.

☯

I was numerous figures of time at the flumes.

J. Michael Yates

I watched the portions hiss from height to stream until watched and watcher fused and appeared one thing.

In recall, trees arise again over war-killed slopes of thought to supervise gravity bearing me, part after part, mostly water, back down to water, compounding with all other flux of lux: the grand translation of the works into the mother tongue of endlessly abiding sea.

I am learning slowly to prefer there were never trees, no hand, no tool to hew them down, never water, never dangerous ways down inscribed by rampaging gravity.

I focus on the cool, smooth flumes: the light upon their lines which bear nothing between nowhere and nowhere.

What I need is what I have but no longer see.

Satana, the cryogene, so easily outstares time at the heatless heart of Hell.

☯

The doors of gods are closed tight tonight.

Trestles of law, beneath their weight of revision, collapse.

Like those of mortal order, the doors of gods are, tonight, tightly closed.

☯

The golden goose-horn of eternity.

Pilgrim, make your peace with Time or seize scrotum and honk the heavens deafeningly.

☯

I have availed myself of heat, of light, near the blaze of your big burning.

Gratefully.

But when your awaited sinking comes, as your unusual vessel detaches from its wharf of unbroken floating,

As you extinguish, as you go down light by light. I intend to be a long, long darkness away.

·

Here at the frontier, it turns suddenly the wrong weather for those who fear darkness most during the day.

·

Indeed there is a personal god up there. And nosey.

A god of love triangulates on hate for love of useless symmetry.

Only poets, the sonofabitch hates, more than it hates poetry.

·

Interregnum between the twin lanterns of dusk and dawn.

Between what it has come to and what it might have been.

How long is the dark, Dad?

Sleep as fast as you can.

Mind well-balanced on one leg: old heron, an older swamp, both dozing.

At some point, all tropes turn and vanish. Somewhere. The words, quite simply, must stop.

Somewhere.

·

J. Michael Yates

Toward pure purpose:

To pound this icy stake of shape through the brass heartworks of snicking time.

❂

Newcomer, take note of this: here the drunken eagle flies with impunity.

Who banishes himself to north necessarily leaves behind all state occasions of the mind.

❂

A cage of white mainland birds, long captive, unexpectedly freed. Will, thus, releases will. Releases. A will letting go. Will releasing.

❂

These words against the darkness from which these words are carved.

❂

These silences against the black fire inside which all silence forges.

❂

So gracefully silent eternity shrills silence at the tiny, temporal thrash.

❂

The situation of fishing explains me: my high-seas trawlers, the big draggers, ravaging my seafloors; my seine-boats with their transparent nets of consciousness, ceaselessly sifting aqueous space; fewer and fewer the gillnetters now; and so with the solo trollers, their gear suggestive of seabirds drying their wings.

This persists: one man clinging to a cliff-face over the water, spear drawn. Waiting. Forever, if necessary.

❂

HONGYUN

Gale winter raindark and only this wharf not listing.

Someplace in the distance, the very distance is listening.

☯

I was up foreword. She was in the galley fixing the grub. The campstove flared. I could see fire through the windshield of the troller and hurried back. When I put it out with the extinguisher, I looked around to say something. She was gone. Must have lit out for the aft of the boat and run overboard. Eight-knot current there in the channel.

Too damn cold. Up here no one learns how to swim. We can't marry within the band. Had to go to Alaska to find her.

☯

A hamper of white mainland birds suddenly freed: Will releases, releases. The will releasing.

☯

She spent the time of her life insular, deliberating what might be worthy of her time.

☯

Because north is nearest nothing, again and again I come back, searching. This is the country where souls, more and more foreign to one another, dwell in uneasy exile.

☯

The glare sea of excess truth now surrounds my used residue of mystery: it has closed it to all other unknowns and continues closing. By the instant, my inside island is less. I am the next ice age advancing.

☯

J. Michael Yates

It is said it was a death-drive

Extincted us

All prodded, stupid, bewildered,

Gregarious into the sea. Also said:

Haida hunters shot the remaining two.

Some say we were

The only mammal native here,

Whatever native comes to mean.

Now gone

And everywhere

As only things long gone can do.

We await your arrival

At a place you once dreamt up in fright.

Yours truly,

The Dawson Caribou.

☯

I am

Where lost things go

Until they are

And never

Found.

☯

The fire which has been burning toward me forever has arrived. And passed. In the ash within this moving skin, no bird stirs.

☯

He lived beneath the tyranny of a massive memory. As he died he watched—with a universal grin—galaxies go out: one by three by ten.

☯

Portrait of my fingerprints upon a snowy massif. And my fingerprints absent.

☯

Tigerine stripes of first light across the dark moss rainforest floor.

J. Michael Yates

I AM ALIVE

At a place of three-minded water,

Of nearby river,

Of circular sea,

Of the curved and arabesquing slough.

The slough keeps memory of river,

Of uplands, of blinding light upon the glaciers

Of turquoise crevasse

Which darkens the faller down to death

And waits beneath a fragile bridge of snow.

Of these high, forever snows,

The river knows.

The slough knows what the river knows. And more:

The slow content of its circles receives from the sea

And adds that knowledge to the river it used to be.

In river and sound very different lives surround.

HONGYUN

The great swan which bugles south from the Arctic

Chooses neither river nor sound but slough

To winter in its proximal distance.

The slough is not emerald like the river.

Nor slate blue like the sea.

Its whiskey-coloured waters go peat

With saline ferment and

Green marsh grass turned sog and brown.

The slough differs from other waters

As the swan differs from other animals which fly.

The swan stands and splays wings over the slough

As Mount Tantalus opens over the corridor below.

J. Michael Yates

When the thing that lives takes wing,

Let it do so like a white swan

Silhouetted against dark mountains

Rising and trumpeting like Gabriel

As it goes.

As its travelling shadow goes

Over Castle Rock which can be

Seen from below

Only against mist

Or fresh dusting of snow,

The town disappearing behind

Out of sight, out of hearing

It is no bad thing

To have been

Close to a town for a time

Then gone.

☯

Don't slam the screen door of the dream as you leave.

DURING: A BOOK OF INTERROGATIVES

"Writing is like riding a drunken lion through the streets." — *CHARLIE BUKOWSKI*

"Happy? I'd rather put my band on the back of a truck, pull it up to playgrounds, and play for kids than play in these smoky clubs. When something happy happens, I'll cut everybody playing happy. Until then, I'll be playing what's happening." — *CHARLES MINGUS*

"The audience...they are the enemy. They are always the enemy." — *JIMMY BUFFET*

"Thinking is the enemy of creativity." — *RAY BRADBURY*

"Wish I didn't know now what I didn't know then." — *BOB SEAGER*

It must speak of things

Which go quickly

Through shadows of consciousness

Like small animals in the thicket

You cannot quite

Be sure you've seen.

☯

The ideal reader of poetry is a great poet who has made a pact with himself never to write poetry for reasons which are none of my business.

☯

J. Michael Yates

Poetry pays less than crime which is said not to pay at all, and it is not necessary to sell more ass than one will ever afford to buy back.

❧

I am an entertainer, not a bearer of truth.

❧

For me, an image is one of an infinite number of entrances to an arena where something ineffable has always been going on. If the thing I pursue could be stated, probably it would be better said in expository prose. The targets most often chosen by good poetry, fiction, and drama call for use of the silences between and behind words. When attempting to evoke what cannot be said, metaphor and indirection are the best engines.

With each piece, I try to cause a structure, a system of images whose parts belong dissonantly to a whole whose meaning cannot be explained. I mean Stravinsky's dissonance, dissonance as a transitional element. Consonance must be achieved one way or the other: Onstage or inside the audient. I give the reader the "thing" I intend to evoke frame by frame, and ask him to project it inside him in the manner that most entertains him. Different and isolate as each of us is, it seems the only honesty.

Ideally, fifteen intelligent readers will make fifteen very different (and fifteen equally justifiable) poems from a piece I have written. As I'm different from you at any moment, I differ from myself through successive moments; even the most familiar things change with the permutations of the coordinates of space/time consciousness. I couldn't possibly (because of the relationships between time, experience, and memory) recreate longitude and latitude of the consciousness which produced a given piece and thereby tell you "what" it means. I couldn't have told you when I was writing it.

Ideally, a reader would come to a poem or story relaxed, with open consciousness, without preconceptions, and without suspicion that the poem is a locked door and someone somewhere—probably the treacherous bastard author—is hiding the key. The parts of a poem which persist inside a reader arrive there via his personal correspondences. Exterior interpretations remain merely exterior.

Belief in one's own associations is very, very difficult, and demands great courage. But only those associations will translate a work of literature from "mine" to "yours".

Ideally, one would read a poem as if he were the first reader ever to read a poem—and as if no one on earth were reading a poem at that moment. Impossible. Necessary.

After having read everything and transferred it from intellect to blood: Ideally, I write as if no one had ever written before. As if no one were writing now. Ridiculous. Imperative.

Understanding is a sweet, vague Renaissance dream which didn't come true. According to me, works of art are not to be understood, but responded to. Understanding promises universal truth. Naïve. I'm a rare user and no pusher of either reality or its ism. I don't assume a "representative universe." As if one could come to an understanding about such things.

Any measure of art is necessarily negative. Failure is the dark side of art's moon. Regardless the phase or brightness of the moon present to the eye, the cold, lightless hemisphere is everpresent and always in full phase. Inevitably intuition is out of synch with its rendering in form because intuition is alive and in motion and form is a condition of arrest. One continues committing form after form notwithstanding. The challenge the poet places before himself is refinement of fraud. How perfectly can he conceal the terrible differential between head and page?

J. Michael Yates

☯

Poetry is about those things for which there are no words.

☯

In literary art, the first word is arbitrary, all which follow are absolute.

☯

Each piece has its own built-in rules. It plays by its own rules and those only.

☯

Style entails learning the rules perfectly and breaking them magnificently.

☯

A great artist is a puzzle maker, not a puzzle solver, except insofar as he must solve problems to do with the structure of the puzzle.

☯

I am a maker of Swiss cheeses. All exits and entrances.

☯

I have no beliefs. Only hypotheses as classically defined: a working statement subject to change in view of better evidence.

I have no heroes, either.

☯

A poet enters maturity when all of his insurance policies against failure lapse and it does not occur to him to renew them.

☯

It is the lantern swinging too slowly between the word and the light.
It is the lantern swinging too slowly between the world and the light.
It is the light swinging too slowly between the world and the word.

❦

All time to write is stolen time. Ultimately, there is nothing in the landscape of living that does not begrudge time to write.

❦

Inside a small garrison of scarcely tolerable words, I barricade and ready myself for a last skirmish with consciousness. Through the silences between words, much poisonous wind—wind of the merely human—streams in. Breath cannot possibly hold.

❦

The entertainment of others is a side-effect of the narcotic we call "creative consciousness."

❦

Less than world art is far, far less than art.

❦

To become a great artist, one must enter obsession which is a shade of madness. This is not presently grounds for institutionalizing the artist, unfortunately.

❦

An artist is responsible for all monsters: both intentional and accidental.

❦

The only redeeming attribute of the human mind is its capacity to change.

❦

J. Michael Yates

Don't jolt the fucking reader by ignorance or by accident.

☯

Madness explains everything. Also, it so baffles those who come into contact with it that it is never noticed that it excuses nothing.

☯

Among elements of form and value, music is the first priority. Resolution of the sensory image next. An idea for a poem may live with me for years, but, usually, the music must declare itself before the real work gets underway.

☯

The world is nouns. The only way you can relate them to one another is with the use of verbs. All else is folly.

☯

There are numberless histories of battles and wars. There are no histories of peace.

☯

War is a game. The most dangerous game is the mind, the consciousness, versus itself.

☯

There is much we can do with electricity, gods, and art without knowing what they are.

☯

Rilke says that a very great poet will write three great lines in a lifetime. Not three great poems, three great lines. I feel I am still pursuing one verb of one of those lines.

☯

How to liberate a sculpture from a marble blank leaving a rubble of chips is one more way of expressing the dilemma of fulfilling the responsibilities of art and living simultaneously.

⚬

Part of greatness is patience. About two centuries of patience. It takes that long to determine whether a poet wasted his life.

⚬

If you stare long enough into an abyss, it will stare back. After indeterminate patience and silence, it will begin, without words, to speak. Listen closely. Although you will never directly communicate that knowledge, it is the only truth you will ever apprehend in cold honesty.

⚬

To grow obsessed by the detail of your environment is to forget that it is there for you to live within.

⚬

It is necessary to loosen and warm up the mind muscles before heading for the front to navigate the metaphor machine where true and untrue prevarications meet.

⚬

I know better than anyone what language cannot do.

⚬

It is much too easy, by accident, to blow out the lantern of what one has learned in the darkness of what he has not.

⚬

The greatest of artists died like dogs without ever understanding that they offended. They looked like humans, talked like humans, and therefore were expected to behave like humans, but could not.

J. Michael Yates

Every genuine artist is obsessive.

Art is a verdict. It says I want you and I will have all of you anytime I wish.

The metaphor machine creates and perpetuates itself. At the same time, there is an anti-metaphor machine whose sole purpose is to put obstacles in the way of writing. The creative mind then creates a device to counter the anti-metaphor machine which maims writing. This regressus ad infinitum occupies the lifetime. Add to this the responsibilities of being human and the game becomes very dangerous: to the sanity of the artist, and to those within his sphere.

☯

The metaphor machine is never off. Invisible fingers test the fabric of all conversation, everything seen, everything perceived.

☯

I never met an artist who didn't experience a sense of outside-ness, of fraud at human occasions.

☯

Our books might be more intelligent than we.

☯

The more I write the more I write.

☯

Everything but the process of writing is prostitution and even that is somewhat in question.

☯

I have always felt that Valéry is probably right in *MONSIEUR TESTE*: to commit the aurora borealis of association to words is an atrocious falsification of the vision.

HONGYUN

❧

A work of art is not dead until all those works of art it has influenced have vanished.

❧

Long ago I abandoned hope that words might be used in the employ of direct communication. As great sculpture shapes the space around it, I use words only to shape (to frame) silences, to catalyze sense of the ineffable. (to intimate the ineffable)

❧

Nomenclature of great Literature: Threat. The reader must subconsciously fear the depth and width and destructive potential of the mind speaking through the cage of words. Art gives neither comfort, congratulation, nor consolation. Great Art—especially comedy—must summon a weather of danger.

❧

Loyalty to my aesthetic—which metamorphoses constantly—is my supreme morality.

❧

Humour	Horror
Idea	Feeling

The viscera of all art is tension. In the case of literature, this is achieved by the polarity between any two of the above elements of the diagram. The greatest word-art is held together by the arcs firing between all four. We call greeting card verse "sentimental" when the onus of feeling is at odds with its vehicle. This pejorative can be taken further. Hitchcock's Psycho is "sentimental" because no other element counterweighs its "Horror."

If Evolution is credible, then all of man's defilement of his own habitat and those of all other components of mass (both animate and inanimate) on this planet, we must accept that this is his natural behaviour. As failure is built into the structures of art, destruction is part of man's evolutionary nomenclature. It is neither unnatural nor abnormal. The urge to destroy is as much an evolutionary matter as our mammalian circulatory system. However, if he were capable only of destruction, the act would not be called destruction and bear the freight of pejorative that it does. We notice most readily the unusual. There would be nothing to notice. Without creation, we would be without measure of destruction. In the situation of no non-destroying, real and feigned guilt would be absent; everywhere everyone would be doing the same thing—in pristine innocence. Curious about the form/chaos, Apollo/Dionysus, Ego/Super-ego, destruction/creation polarity is that another of man's evolutionary dimensions is his unfortunate capacity to register his desecration. If only no conception of synthesis were possible, the species could continue toward its extinction with perfect peace of mind. Knowledge that vision of the artificial is but a dimension of the natural is the difference between intelligence and wisdom.—THE QUALICUM PHYSICS

Poetry is most definitely not what was lost in translation. Regardless the consensus of the degree of greatness of a piece, the poem was never in any language in the first place. Poetry is what was lost when the shadow of intuitive motion entered the cage of words.

If to translate is to bring the distant nearer, a literal rendering from one language to another is the opposite of translation. Resonances are never identical in any two languages. Only the Geist of the work may be almost transferred.

HONGYUN

That one cannot see at once what one writes and what one writes about is a battleship made of drunken white mice.

❧

Metaphor is usually taken up as a weapon against the adversary, absence. Often it takes until the handle of the weapon has worn smooth by the callous it created that the wielder notices the engine itself is the enemy.

❧

"...irrealism, not antirealism or unrealism—is all I would confidently predict is likely to characterize the prose fiction of the 1970's. I welcome this...because unlike those critics who regard realism as what literature has been aiming at all along, I tend to regard it as a kind of aberration in the history of literature." — JOHN BARTH

❧

Discussion of absolutes is poor consolation for being denied their existence, but allowed capacity to conceive them.

❧

Figuratively: Observation of sentimental taboos, of rituals which demonstrate one's "good citizenship," physiological commands, and other detail of physical survival are chattels of one's Supreme Being. The only property of art in which an artist can afford honest interest—process—belongs to dominion of a Supreme Doing. Product necessarily passes into the hands of the other world and there whores away according to the whims of the lords of literary industry.

Process, the eternally astounding, alien, intuitive buzz in the yonder of consciousness which triggers form; process transports a maker to the most intense purity his mental tolerances dare permit—and sometimes beyond to temporary or irreversible disaster. The sanctity of process is fragile from the outset and grows increasingly more so the deeper one loses himself in the labyrinth of consciousness. It can be argued that, for all purposes relating to the artist, a work begins

J. Michael Yates

to obsolesce the instant the pen touches the blank page. If an artist consciously allows any exterior judgment, at face value, positive or negative, to alter his aesthetic base, he has profaned his already imperfect purity, broken faith with his only reliable mode of reflexive communication. The lion, traditionally first to feed on his own aesthetic kill, has given ground to hyenas, vultures, and the flies. If he has been, until now, a responsible artist, he has forgotten how to be. Having savaged the integrity of his doing, his continued existence seems to me indefensible. This is not to say that consciousness has nothing to do with exterior phenomena, including judgments from the exterior. It is to say that perceptions and concepts must undergo process before they become the stuff of art. Art does not tolerate aesthetic hand-me-downs innocently, ingenuously. By dismantling an idea and reassembling as though it had never before been synthesized, the artist legitimately puts claim; he has but to translate it from the tongues of intellect to blood-language (dissolve it so thoroughly that intellect no longer recognizes its previous face) and put it to work without awareness that this event is transpiring under his very nose.

❧

At kitsch level, the platitude, "A picture is worth a thousand words" is more or less tenable. Confessing an unzealous bias, it seems to me rather sad that so few pictures are worth even a single silence.

❧

PROPOSITION: The creative impulse can be said to be almost totally original. The same cannot be said of that impulse rendered into form.

❧

A genuine artist, like a resolute suicide, will find a way to find his way eventually.

❧

Anti-art relates to art as anti-matter does to matter. A mirrorism. It must not be confused with the opposite of form. It seems to me the greatest single example of anti-art in literary history is Gongora's "Sonnet on Writing a Sonnet."

☯

Each time another corpse of disastrous event arrives to be chilled among others in my mnemonic morgue, the focal-length of the lens I turn toward the world lengthens. The illusory third dimension withers proportionately.

☯

With the proviso that money is not a measure of quality in art—a premise that most will not grant—, an artist becomes a professional the instant he can say so to himself and believe it.

POSTULATE: One attempts to write the literature he would most like to read. From at least one standpoint, I can argue that I disapprove of all the literature I have ever read, including my own. But I am interested in three or four pieces which I have not yet written.

☯

Experience: Most set forth with their few coins of time to purchase the valences of guilt, but sell out to mere innocence of innocence.

☯

And now only death remains between me and my dying.

☯

There should be difference between cardinal and ordinal terminations. One should prefer.

☯

Only death speaks to all questions of freedom. I am death: Freedom is a far more bewildering incarceration than actual imprisonment.

☯

205

J. Michael Yates

Black and white translate to gray which translates to neither.

❡

An artist who triangulates by what he has made instead of by what he has not: isn't.

❡

The eye misrepresents the seen, the brain misrepresents the eye, the word falsifies the brain, and I had nothing to do with it, despite the false impression that I have survived. I am is not: *nicht schültig, alle Punkten.*

❡

To those who hope art finds its purpose in cleansing the skunk of time from the uniform of eternity: Our best is translation of scent to sound or sight and, occasionally, one might conceal the stench of one within the stench of the other for a little while.

❡

In the whole of the human experience, only art is of a magnitude of useless seriousness sufficient to warrant what Hesse in *Steppenwolf* calls "high Mozartian laughter."

❡

It is very important to declare. It is imperative to renounce all declarations regularly. It is far, far too easy to intend an entrance and produce a wall.

❡

It is a very long haul through terrains of present, past, future, variant texts, translators, all philosophy, mirages of the rational, dim phosphorescence of intuitive certainty, Zeno, Bergson, trial, experience (overdeveloped sense of the invulnerable absences) to the intermittent destination that Herakleitos and Parmenides are two names to summon the very same mind.

HONGYUN

❧

Art forms are, at best, diversionary engines. Their glitter draws attention from the deadly warfare of consciousness against all limits — all of which, ultimately, reveal themselves self-imposed.

❧

If creative consciousness could be measured, it would have to be in terms of its obsessive capacities. If creative consciousness could be measured, it would have to be in terms of its associational precision, the velocity. If creative consciousness could be measured, it would have to be in terms of its inability to accept the textures of experience at surface value.

❧

The young literatus lives in an *als ob* world. The auditory and visual silences between and behind words and lines do not present themselves to him as tools of communication. Our present languages of science, of the arts, of religion are not engineered to deliver "things as they are." For this, the history of consciousness must answer.

❧

In my twenties, any apparent uncertainty was fraudulent. Now, many educations later, my uncertainty is authentic.

❧

To write with what I consider responsibility is to place one's sanity on the line. On every line.

❧

If a denominator common to all literary theorists, critics, linguists, scholars, and reviewers is possible, it must be some permutation of this: All share a mandate to reduce to the lowest possible terms that which the artist has accepted as the irreducible.

❧

J. Michael Yates

CONTAINER AND CONTAINED: The hand of form must clasp the hand of energy as if Dionysus and Apollo had never before made open acquaintance. Primal fusion. It is extremely difficult to ignore knowledge that what we accept as chaos is very distant from perfect absence of form, that we apply form to the stratified wreckages of all previous forms strewn over the dusk of history.

☯

UNCLUTTERED JEOPARDY: Failure as a consequence of a supreme effort is never a disgrace. I prefer that failure to the diminutive survivals which arrive via the offices of caution in reward for low risk existence.

☯

Like amateurs, feckless professional writers are of nuisance value only.

☯

It is healthy for an artist to fear what he most wants. Human imagination is so indigent he stands in dreadful jeopardy of realizing it.

☯

Effectively, a poem is poor taxidermy of intuitive event. Like history, art-forms are accessories after events. Translation of an intuitive comet into form is to transfer the dynamic to the static. The greatest works of art are those which offer the largest measure of illusory motion.

☯

For most, pleasure pertains only to those lives which go on from the nose downward. It cannot be demonstrated that consciousness exceeds the routine in desirability. Few are sufficiently conscious to note that consciousness and routine are not one. I conclude that the object of consciousness is total synchronicity of circumstance, arrangement and action. At the moment we can only approach this to the point of immediate history.

HONGYUN

❀

Great literature and threat: The reader must subconsciously fear the depth, width, and destructive capacity of the mind speaking in his direction from a damaged cage of words.

❀

Comedy, especially, must summon a weather of danger.

❀

Art gives neither comfort, congratulation, nor consolation.

❀

Art gives neither truth nor wisdom. The best art fangles silence or space in such a manner that members of a creative audience may invest the form with as many truths as there are members of a creative audience.

❀

I have no politics. The well-tailored stuff of history has never presented itself in a pattern which approached the adequate, let alone the satisfactory. I'm surprised those who belong to and voluntarily work for political parties—nourished by only idealism and water. Politicians, at least, have something to gain—hence their singleness of purpose.

❀

The very notion of mortality obliterates the worth of art both as process and product. Especially product.

❀

In Miller's *THE MISFITS*, Eli Wallach says to Marilyn Monroe: "I can't land, and I can't get up to God." I like the line despite the *Duino Elegies* smell of it. In my experience, a disciplined consciousness has no intermediate (read moderate) gears. Once

J. Michael Yates

blooded to the metaphor, it cannot be recalled until the quarry has been treed or slain. Consciousness is capable of near-absolute inertia of rest and near-absolute inertia of motion. Nothing between those two poles. I think that most artists assault consciousness because there is no switch which reads OFF. Once airborne (beyond a certain stage of consciousness-addiction), the metaphor machine can only crash-land: booze, drugs, sex, exercise, whatever works.

☯

Address to the apparent: Over a horizon to horizon plain of No, an infrequent mirage which resembles Yes.

☯

Dauer im Wechsel, usw.: With the application of consciousness, Heraclitos and Parmenides become interchangeable, become minor variations on a major theme of impossibility.

☯

Imagination is the shadow of a lone gull in passage between sun and the running roof-tops of the sea.

☯

The situation of the contemporary artist is somewhat like that of the builder who attempts to erect structures on artificial property created by compacting refuse for fill. I confess a nostalgic longing for encounter of primal energy and primal form: the first struggle between Dionysus and Apollo against and for one another. Both energy and form have gone diluent. We erect forms not on solid ground but on towering middens of ruined previous forms. There is no place to bury them. As for energy: The quality of energy improves only in direct proportion to the quality of form.

☯

Not only to know, but to know that one knows—then to comprehend the ultimate impotence of knowing. There should be occasional dispensation from this. And frequent conversations with Socrates.

At first, a prophet refuses the mission to execute the directives issued by his god. At first. Never in transit. Never at last.

The random. Noah's Ark was built to float, not to sail. It was without sail, without helm, without rudder. No one navigated because the landmarks by which a captain might discern where he is not were gone.

If I am created in the image of a god, that god is a jinxed and bewildered herd.

It seems that body lends life to the mind and repossesses without notice.

Rapture of the shallows: the best-loved malady of realism.

All art is pun. Without the walls made of words, images, and noise against which to ricochet, no pun, no art would be possible.

Poetry is an art of mysterious disappearances.

Polarity is not of opposings. It is completion.

J. Michael Yates

Fireflies of certainty lead us on the endless death dance through the dark.

☯

For most purposes of consciousness (that of the artist), a literary work dies the instant that the pen-point enters contact with the page.

☯

Larceny is a high-priority component of every maker's survival kit.

☯

Whence a judgment? The editors judge. No, they are accountable to their sources of funds. They're all dying of democracies: by region, by nation, by language, by sex, by ethnos, by genre, etc. Then reviewers. No, too ignorant, too whimsical, too easy to corrupt. Fellow writers? Never. Built into the aesthetic of a responsible artist is a necessary logic which declares that if his own poetic is correct, all others must be incorrect. Regardless the resemblance. Family and friends, surely. Honesty is inimical to the concepts of family and friendship. Their bias is lethal. The writer himself. Since he cannot acknowledge peers, it would seem so, but no: he knows better than any his consciousness is prototype, erratic, contrary, and indolent. Better than any he knows that the maker's consciousness is the last faculty to be charged with such an important task.

☯

Since consciousness can rarely be summoned, I must be on call at all times.

☯

Every powerful religion has been essentially an attitude toward property. Which is to say, toward something. Every powerful aesthetic has been essentially an attitude (as form) toward nothing.

☯

There was a time, possibly, when reason, with sufficient faith and energy could transport me—seemingly— anywhere. But then I was too young to imagine a great deal of anywhere. Now all the voluptuous anywheres have vanished and only the ghost of reason abides—an abused toy to serve idle argument (between projects) when competent conversation lags.

"Detail is the business of scholarship, not learning." I think Kerr said that. To check it out would be to diminish the value of the observation.

While scholars are probably the legitimate custodians (administrators) of the history of literature, these same people (for reasons of pressure, bad education, bad taste, money, worship of obscurity, and indigence of imagination) fashion ways to give many a well-croaked author and many a well-croaked book the appearance of being alive. These life-support systems are extremely effective; so effective, in fact, that there is virtually no space available for living writers on the literary stage. Contemporary writers would work much harder if they knew they were being watched. Pull the plug.

Schopenhauer's trope of genius as a hare; while alive it can only be shot at; it cannot be eaten until dead. All well and good: the dead don't complain when one misrepresents them. Presently, over the landscape of contemporary world literature, there hangs a toxic silence. Earlier on, there was gunfire. Rolling closer.

I've found it very difficult to learn to resist memorization of my own lines. But necessary. Not only does it waste valuable writing time; more importantly, it imperils the impetus to revise. Rote is a loan-shark. It demands outrageous interest for its tiny investment.

J. Michael Yates

☯

When imagination starves or for some other reason subsides, disease sets in. One commences feeding it falsifications of personal history incompetently remembered.

☯

An acquaintance approaches me on the street. I say: Hello. He says: Fine. If I could get to the heart of that event, I might learn one small truth about language.

☯

Language can not bear the weight of the best of human experience. It offers only flat clichés like love, grief, hate, etc. which can not be modulated toward meaning by other words—except in the most primitive uses: "Hey! Watch out." Dogs can do that.

ABOUT THE AUTHOR

J. Michael Yates was born in the Ozark Mountains of Missouri and did graduate degrees at the Universities of Missouri and Michigan. He is a widely published author of poetry, fiction, drama, translations, and philosophical essays. He has edited several anthologies and several literary magazines. His work has been translated into most of the western languages and several of the eastern ones and his drama for radio, television, and stage have been produced both nationally and internationally. His last rank as a university professor was Distinguished Professor.

He has won many literary prizes including the Major Hopwood Awards (both poetry and drama the same year) and the Lifetime Achievement Award in the Arts and Sciences from University of Missouri.

He has also been a logger, a powder monkey, a motorcycle racer, a broadcasting executive, a broadcaster, an advertising executive, a print salesman, a commercial photographer, a publisher. He retired after seventeen years as a Maximum Security Prison Guard and SWAT team member. Now, he and his wife teach languages, history of ideas, and science in their home in Vancouver.

Printed in the United States
29275LVS00004B/61-117